FLOYD CLYMER'S MOTORCYCLIST'S LIBRARY

The Book of the
NSU QUICKLY

A Practical Handbook covering all models

R. H. Warring

ANNOUNCEMENT

By special arrangement with the original publishers of this book, Sir Isaac Pitman & Son, Ltd., of London, England, we have secured the exclusive publishing rights for this book, as well as all others in THE MOTORCYCLIST'S LIBRARY.

Included in THE MOTORCYCLIST'S LIBRARY are complete instruction manuals covering the care and operation of respective motorcycles and engines; valuable data on speed tuning, and thrilling accounts of motorcycle race events. See listing of available titles elsewhere in this edition.

We consider it a privilege to be able to offer so many fine titles to our customers.

FLOYD CLYMER
Publisher of Books Pertaining to Automobiles and Motorcycles

2125 W. PICO ST.   LOS ANGELES 6, CALIF.

INTRODUCTION

Welcome to the world of digital publishing ~ the book you now hold in your hand, while unchanged from the original edition, was printed using the latest state of the art digital technology. The advent of print-on-demand has forever changed the publishing process, never has information been so accessible and it is our hope that this book serves your informational needs for years to come. If this is your first exposure to digital publishing, we hope that you are pleased with the results. Many more titles of interest to the classic automobile and motorcycle enthusiast, collector and restorer are available via our website at www.VelocePress.com. We hope that you find this title as interesting as we do.

NOTE FROM THE PUBLISHER

The information presented is true and complete to the best of our knowledge. All recommendations are made without any guarantees on the part of the author or the publisher, who also disclaim all liability incurred with the use of this information.

TRADEMARKS

We recognize that some words, model names and designations, for example, mentioned herein are the property of the trademark holder. We use them for identification purposes only. This is not an official publication.

INFORMATION ON THE USE OF THIS PUBLICATION

This manual is an invaluable resource for the classic motorcycle enthusiast and a "must have" for owners interested in performing their own maintenance. However, in today's information age we are constantly subject to changes in common practice, new technology, availability of improved materials and increased awareness of chemical toxicity. As such, it is advised that the user consult with an experienced professional prior to undertaking any procedure described herein. While every care has been taken to ensure correctness of information, it is obviously not possible to guarantee complete freedom from errors or omissions or to accept liability arising from such errors or omissions. Therefore, any individual that uses the information contained within, or elects to perform or participate in do-it-yourself repairs or modifications acknowledges that there is a risk factor involved and that the publisher or its associates cannot be held responsible for personal injury or property damage resulting from the use of the information or the outcome of such procedures.

WARNING!

One final word of advice, this publication is intended to be used as a reference guide, and when in doubt the reader should consult with a qualified technician.

Preface

SOME time after the introduction of the S/23, S/2 23 and F 23 models NSU Motorenwerke of Neckarsulm, Germany took the decision to cease production of two-wheelers in order to concentrate on a rationalized programme of car production. These models were, therefore, the last vehicles of the Quickly series. Revisions and additions have been made in the present Edition to cover the specifications of the 23-inch wheel models more comprehensively, so that this present volume does in fact describe all the Quickly models produced in their complete production run of some thirteen years.

There is no doubt that Quickly mopeds will continue to be seen on the roads for some years to come, and home maintenance and home servicing is an even more vital factor for Quickly owners. Additional notes describe the present (1969) position as regards spares, which are no longer as readily obtainable as they were some four years or so ago. This book therefore represents one of the few readily available sources of information on the NSU Quickly moped, whatever its age or model.

It should perhaps be stressed that the Quickly owner does not have to be a mechanic to carry out normal maintenance work on his (or her) machine —nor even to carry out such jobs as decarbonizing, relining brakes and attending to other matters which may become necessary after a period of use. The Quickly, in fact, is a very simple machine—easily stripped right down, if necessary—and even detailed maintenance can be learnt as you go.

The early chapters in this book are mainly elementary in nature, describing the workings of the machine in simple terms, regular maintenance and "trouble shooting." The sections on detailed maintenance (Chapter 5) give all the information necessary for complete stripping, etc., for those owners who may wish to attempt major overhauls.

R. H. W.

Contents

CHAP.		PAGE
1. PRODUCTION OF THE NSU QUICKLY	. . . . .	1
2. GENERAL DESCRIPTION AND HANDLING	. . . .	4
3. REGULAR MAINTENANCE	. . . . . .	29
4. FAULT FINDING		39
5. DETAILED MAINTENANCE	. . . . . .	42

    1. Cables and Controls
    2. Front and Rear Brakes
    3. Wheels
    4. Suspension, Frame and Forks
    5. Chain
    6. Carburettor and Air Filter
    7. Magneto/Generator
    8. Engine Unit
    9. Replacement of Engine Parts
    10. Decarbonizing
    11. Sources of Trouble

6. ELECTRICAL EQUIPMENT	. . . . .	90
APPENDIX 1: SPECIFICATION	. . . . . .	97
APPENDIX 2: DESIGN CHANGES		102
APPENDIX 3: MODEL COMPONENTS	. . . .	106
APPENDIX 4: SPECIAL TOOLS .	. . .	109
Index		111

1 Production of the NSU Quickly

THE NSU Quickly is a German-made machine—the NSU standing for the South German town of Neckarsulm, where the factory is situated. NSU, in fact, was Germany's largest manufacturer of mopeds, motor-cycles and motor-scooters, and of motor-cycle, four-stroke and two-stroke engines.

Pressed-steel Frame. When production started again on motor-cycles after World War II, a number of new design ideas were incorporated, notably the employment of a pressed-steel beam frame in place of the more conventional welded-up tubular frame. To do this demanded the employment of very heavy and costly equipment for the cutting out or "blanking" of sheet steel pieces and then forming them into a hollowed or sectioned shape for welding together. Superior performance is claimed for this type of construction, e.g. greater rigidity and strength, better appearance, etc., the main reason why it is not more universally adopted being the high initial cost of laying down the plant to do the job, especially if an existing production line is scrapped in consequence of the changeover.

The principle of the production of a pressed-steel frame is as follows. Starting with a sheet of steel, two blanks are punched out in a large press. The blanks are then transferred to another press which both shapes them to half-shell form and punches in necessary fixing holes. At another point on the production line the half-shells are joined by welding to complete the basic frame, and the engine bracket, head tube and various other fittings, are welded on. Finally alignment is checked in a special jig and the unit is inspected before being passed on to the paint shop for finishing. After joining the main assembly line the finished frame becomes virtually the backbone of the whole machine to which the various other components are attached. Fig. 1 shows the main assembly around the standard Quickly frame.

The NSU Quickly was introduced in 1953, at a period when there were nearly fifty different manufacturers producing mopeds in Germany, to say nothing of the dozens of other individual manufacturers in the remainder of Continental Europe. It rapidly established itself as the leading German moped and in the space of three years production exceeded the half-million mark. At the height of its popularity, production of Quickly mopeds reached a figure of approximately one thousand *per day*, and at this period fifty per cent of all German exports of mopeds were NSU Quickly machines. Production of two-wheelers by the NSU company in Germany eventually ceased, however, about 1966, the S/23, S/2 23 and F being the last vehicles manufactured in the Quickly series.

British Agents. A British company, NSU (Great Britain) Ltd., was established in 1954 for the import of all NSU machines into this country, with registered offices at 7 Chesterfield Gardens, Curzon Street, London (subsequently moving to Kings House, 10 Haymarket, London, S.W.1). A separate maintenance and spares section was set up at Hammersmith

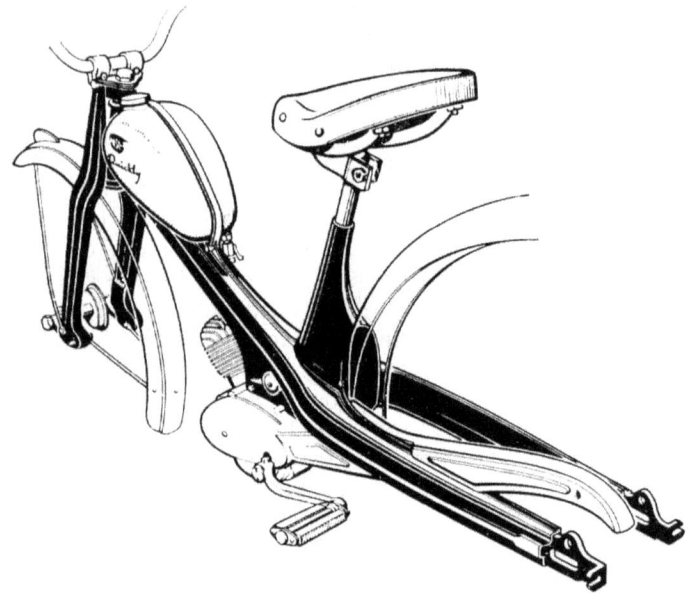

Fig. 1. The NSU Quickly Pressed-steel Frame

London, in 1957 to handle major overhauls and repairs, and facilitate the flow of spares, etc., to NSU agents and dealers. The latter centre is no longer operative as NSU (Great Britain) Ltd. no longer imports two-wheelers.

Spare Parts. Some two thousand authorized NSU Agents and dealers were established throughout the country by 1957, carrying representative stocks of spares as part of their agency agreement. All Quickly spares originated from Germany and many components, e.g. nuts, screws, etc., are of German DIN standard not normally stocked by garages.

With the cessation of production of Quickly mopeds the question of obtaining spares has tended to become a little difficult in particular cases.

PRODUCTION OF THE NSU QUICKLY

Stocks held by the original agents have obviously run down, but a limited number of firms have continued to specialize in Quickly repairs and service, and can supply such spares as are still available. The addresses of such firms can be found from a study of the advertisement pages of the motor-cycling magazines.

Stocks of spares are still held by NSU (Great Britain) Ltd., at their new address of Harbour Way, Shoreham-by-Sea, Sussex (telephone Shoreham-by-Sea 5281), although these are obviously running down.

Apart from the replacement of German standard components—which in the case of nuts, screws, etc., should be obtainable from engineering supply sources—servicing requirements can still be tackled by many garages, or the remaining NSU specialists (as noted above). The Quickly is robustly made and excellently designed, so that apart from normal wear and tear due to age, regular maintenance will generally ensure continued trouble-free running. More detailed maintenance can be tackled on a "replacement" basis, where such parts are available, and in this case can be tackled by anyone without previous mechanical knowledge simply by following the stripping and reassembly instructions given in subsequent chapters. Professional help may be needed, however, in the case where standard replacement parts are not available.

2 General Description and Handling

THREE versions of the NSU Quickly were produced after 1957 around the same basic design. These are the Standard model, also known as the Quickly-N or Quickly Normal (Fig. 2); the Quickly-S (or Special) (Fig. 3); and the Quickly-L or Luxe (Fig. 4).

The N, S, and L are all two-speed machines utilizing an identical engine and gearbox, wheels, etc., and differing only in the amount of

FIG. 2. THE BASIC MODEL—THE QUICKLY-N

fairing and other details. From these developed a series of three-speed machines, again based upon the same engine but with slightly modified porting and increased compression ratio to give more power, and employing a three-speed gearbox.

The first of these—the "Cavallino"—had larger wheels and a complete redesign as regards shapes to give a "motorcycle" appearance and incorporate a number of features usually found on these larger and

Fig. 3. The Quickly-S
This model incorporates slightly more fairing.

Fig. 4. The Quickly-L
This model extends the degree of fairing employed, has redesigned handlebars and sprung rear suspension.

heavier machines. This was followed by the Quickly-T and the Quickly-TT, both again differing considerably in appearance. There was also a Quickly-TTK version of the TT model, which incorporated a kickstarter for the engine.

None of these models became a standard import line to this country. A few Cavallinos were introduced, but were not repeated. Two only of each of the T and TT models were brought into this country by NSU (Great Britain). None of these models, in fact, can be considered as successful production designs although some numbers may be found on the Continent.

From these three-speed models, however, developed the Quickly-S/2, which reverted to the original Quickly design layouts but differs basically

FIG. 4A. THE QUICKLY 23 MODELS
23-N 23-S
23-S/2 23-F

in employing a strengthened frame, larger wheels and hubs with heavy-duty tyres, and is fitted with a dualseat as standard. The engine is still the basic Quickly unit but with increased power as on the other three-speed models, and a three-speed gearbox is fitted. Overall dimensions and general appearance are similar to the S and L models.

The Quickly S/2 was introduced into this country in late 1960 and has proved a particularly popular model. It is free from the troubles and limitations experienced with the earlier three-speed machines and generally similar to the N, S, and L models as regards handling, general maintenance, etc.

A major change was introduced in 1961 with the S/2 23 adopting 23-in. instead of 26-in. wheels, with larger tyres. The new wheel size dictated a change in mudguards and fairings, offering at the same time a chance to

GENERAL DESCRIPTION AND HANDLING

improve the styling—noticeably in the protruding streamlined headlamp and speedometer housing, a larger and completely new tank shape indented for knee grips and the full fairing between the front saddle tube and the rear mudguard.

The S/2 23 was introduced in this country in October 1961 and was followed in October-November 1962 by 23-in. wheel versions of the N and S, designated N/23 and S/23, respectively. These, basically, retain the "mechanics" of the original N and S allied to 23-in. wheels. The S/23 incorporates the new tank and more streamlined styling of the two-seat version whilst the N/23 represents more of a basic conversion of its 26-in. wheel forerunner, differing only in wheel size and revised mudguard shapes and minor details.

From 1961–62 onwards the 23-in. wheel versions became the standard models, with production of the 26-in. wheel original series ceasing although the Quickly-N (26-in. wheel) continued to be available in this country up to the end of 1962.

A further new model—the Quickly F—was introduced in May 1963, this being basically identical to the S/2 23 but with pivoted frame real suspension fitted with two hydraulic shock absorbers.

DIFFERENCE OF MODELS

The Quickly-N is the lowest priced model, supplied with painted where rims and without a speedometer. The Quickly-S has valances on the front and rear mudguards, chrome-plated wheel rims, a side-prop stand and is fitted with a combined mileometer-speedometer in the headlamp as standard. It is finished in a single colour. Otherwise the appearance is identical with the model N.

The Quickly-L has a more widely valanced front mudguard and a completely redesigned rear mudguard which joins to the saddle tube and almost completely encloses the upper half of the rear wheel. A luggage carrier is incorporated in this shape, instead of being separately mounted as on the other two models. A further difference is that the handlebars are made as a pressed-steel unit of channel section in place of the conventional bent tube, with the steering head streamlined in, and appearing much more solid and with control cables led underneath out of sight. The lamp is formed integrally with this head and the mileometer-speedometer is repositioned behind the line of the handlebars. The overall appearance, whilst still retaining the basic Quickly outline, is more in the nature of a motor-scooter than a moped. There is also an improvement in the ride given by the addition of rear suspension which entails a slight change in the rear end of the frame design, whilst the appearance of the front and rear wheels has been enhanced by the adoption of full-width hubs. Dual colour schemes and white sidewall tyres are standard on all Luxe production models.

External differences between the S/2 and the other models can be seen by studying Fig. 4A. Apart from the strengthened frame, the rear mudguard fairing is similar to the S and the front mudguard to the L models. The main difference results from the larger tyres and the twin seat. As regards maintenance, etc., all the descriptions for the N, S, and L models can be taken as applying to the Quickly-S/2. Where there are specific differences these are noted. The standard Quickly engine description also applies, except that there is a different carburettor on the S/2 and, of course, a three-speed gearbox. These are detailed in Figs. 40A and 49A, respectively.

The T, TT, TTK, and Cavallino models are not separately described, since again the descriptions of the N, S, and L generally apply, whilst engine and gearbox details are essentially as for the S/2.

The Quickly-S/2 23 differs from the single-seat 23 in. wheel models in having considerably larger brakes and a heavier (23 × 2½ in.) tyre on the rear wheel. It also has a three-speed gearbox as standard. The Quickly-S/23 model embodies the same modern styling with dirt-protecting valances on the rear mudguard, chromium-plated rims and spokes and streamlined toolbox mounted in the extension fairing between saddle tube and rear mudguard. It has a two-speed gearbox as standard. The Quickly-N 23 model shows less difference compared with its earlier counterpart but is identified by the smaller diameter wheels and larger tyres and deeper mudguards. Like the original N it has painted wheel rims and spokes.

All of the 23-in. wheel models incorporate a stronger centre stand, with a strengthened engine crankcase, and improved lights. Control cables are taken down externally rather than inside the frame section and there are minor differences in the brake linkage. On the S/2 23 the footbrake rod is located on the right-hand side; and on the S 23 and N 23 on the left-hand side. Engine, gearbox, clutch and general engineering details remain the same as for the earlier models and the same descriptions apply, with minor alterations as noted. Beginning in 1963, however, the clutch design was altered and on models from about March 1963 onwards in this country was of the five-plate rather than the three-plate type. The Quickly-F features the same basic layout as the S/2 23 with three-speed gearbox and five-plate clutch as standard, and sprung rear suspension.

TWO-STROKE ENGINE

Apart from detail differences related to these various modifications, all models can be considered identical for the purpose of handling and maintenance.

Engine Cooling. The engine is the same on all models, being a NSU single-cylinder two-stroke unit of 49 c.c. capacity developing a maximum of 1·4 horse-power.* The cylinder is finned and cooled by air blowing past it when the machine is in motion. The finned area is adequate to

* 1·7 horse-power on the S/2 model.

GENERAL DESCRIPTION AND HANDLING 9

dissipate enough heat when the engine is running stationary for it not to overheat in this condition when idling, but prolonged *fast* running of the engine when the machine is stationary is not advisable. Even so, the Quickly engine is far less likely to seize through over-heating than a conventional engine for both the cylinder and piston are made of light alloy and therefore tend to expand equally when hot. The usual cause of seizing on a conventional engine is that the piston is of light alloy and expands at a much faster rate than the surrounding steel cylinder. As a consequence the piston can increase to a size where it "jams" or seizes in the cylinder. Another point in favour of a light alloy cylinder is that aluminium conducts heat more readily than steel, and therefore tends to *lose* heat to the surrounding air more rapidly. The main reason why light alloy cylinders are not employed more is that the metal is normally soft and thus not suitable for a rubbing surface. In the Quickly engine the inside of the cylinder, or bore, is specially treated to give a hardened finish by being chromium-plated.

Two-stroke Principle. The engine operates on the two-stroke principle. That is to say it dispenses with mechanically-operated valves to control the flow of fuel through the engine, and the escape of the exhaust gases. All the necessary timing of the gas flow is done by the movement of the piston up and down the cylinder, which opens and closes openings or ports formed in the cylinder. Thus the operation of the engine is made as simple as possible. Actually there is one valve in the cylinder head, operated by a cable controlled by a small lever on the left-hand handlebar. This is a "decompressor" which, when operated, opens the top of the cylinder to the outside air, through the exhaust port. This prevents compression building up in the cylinder when the engine is turned over and moves the piston to the top of its stroke. Its purpose is to enable the engine to be turned over freely and rapidly by the pedals for starting, and also to stop the engine if opened when running (at idling speed). The pedals are geared up to the engine for the purpose of starting and without this decompressor to "free" the engine, it would be quite hard work to set the motor spinning. More complete details of the engine can be found in Chapter V, Section 8.

Engine Unit. The engine assembly is attached rigidly to the pressed-steel frame by means of three mounting bolts. The complete unit (*see* Figs. 44 and 45) comprises the engine itself; the carburettor, supplying fuel mixture to the engine; the magneto-dynamo, driven by the engine crankshaft and supplying the spark to the spark plug and electricity for the lights and horn; the clutch; the gearbox; and the pedal drive.

Carburettor. The carburettor is a metering device which provides the correct mixture of fuel and air for the engine. Air is drawn through the carburettor by the suction of the piston inside the cylinder. Fuel is added to it and the combustible mixture is sucked into the engine, compressed by the piston inside the cylinder, and ignited by the spark plug. Since the air drawn in might well contain dirt, dust and similar abrasive particles which could cause damage to the inside of the engine, the air intake side of a carburettor is fitted with a filter—merely a form of "sieve," if you like, which traps harmful solid particles and thus allows only clean air to be drawn through it.

On the Quickly, ingenious use is made of the shape of the pressed-steel frame to improve on this. The open underside of the frame tends to trap and direct air on to the filter (Fig. 5). This form of pre-entry passage, it is claimed, effectively smooths the airflow and in so doing causes it to drop much of the solid impurities which may be carried with it before it reaches the filter. Thus there is less work for the filter to do and far less risk of abrasive particles getting inside the engine. This feature is also employed on NSU motor-cycle designs and is stated to reduce piston and cylinder wear by 70–75 per cent.

CLUTCH AND GEARBOX

The engine is connected to the final drive shaft via the clutch and gearbox. The purpose of the clutch is to disconnect the engine from the gearbox for the purpose of changing smoothly from one gear to another. The gearbox provides two different drive ratios,* and also a neutral position where the engine can run disconnected from the final drive.

The basic mechanics of this system are quite easy to understand and knowing *how* it works makes for a better understanding of the operation of the controls. A simplified drawing of the Quickly engine unit is shown in Fig. 6 from which the working of each of the components can be followed.

All we need to know about the engine at this stage is that it has a protruding shaft, called the crankshaft, which rotates at a speed controlled by the throttle setting—this, in effect, varying the amount of fuel fed into the engine and thus making it run faster or slower, at will.

Clutch Plates. The clutch is attached to the end of the crankshaft. In the diagram a very elementary form of clutch is shown for clarity. The Quickly clutch is a little more complicated (*see* Chapter 5, Section 8, Fig. 50) but it works on exactly the same principle. The clutch, as drawn, consists of two flat plates, one with a facing of some frictional material. One plate is movable, that is, it can be drawn back along its shaft by operation of the clutch lever. In this position the two plates are quite free and so the engine crankshaft can rotate driving the one (driving) disc without any connexion with the rest of the mechanism.

* Three speeds on the Quickly-S/2.

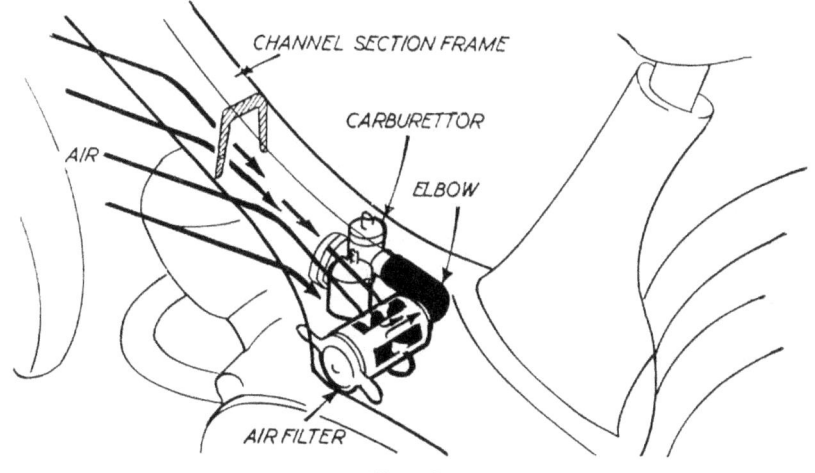

FIG. 5

A diagram showing how the air is trapped in the open channel section of the frame and fed down to the air filter and hence to the carburettor.

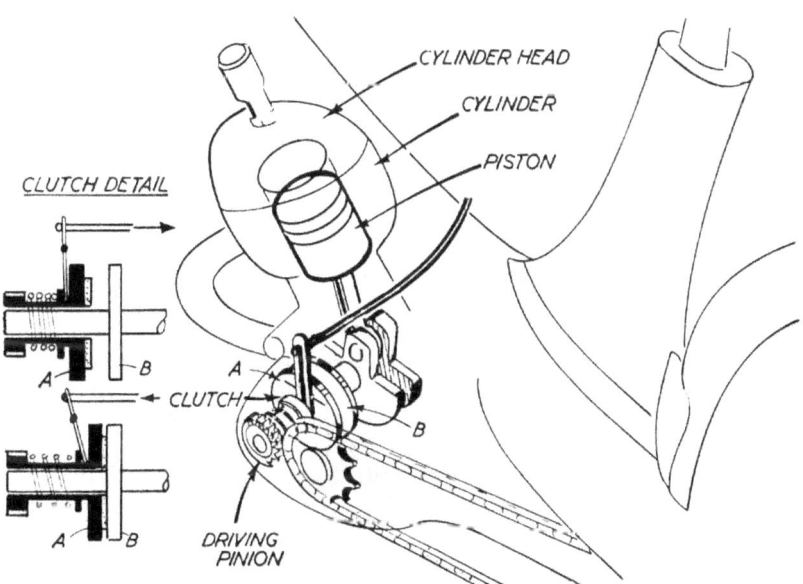

FIG. 6. SIMPLIFIED DIAGRAM OF THE ENGINE UNIT

The clutch is purely diagrammatic to illustrate its action in simple form. Compare with Fig. 50 for actual details of the Quickly clutch.

If the clutch lever is released, however, a strong spring forces the two discs into contact, effectively locking them together solidly (which is where the frictional facing on one of the discs is effective). Now the engine drives both clutch plates as one, and anything else connected to the driven side of the clutch, e.g. the gearbox mainshaft and the rear wheel drive if the latter is in gear.

It will be appreciated that if the driven side of the clutch is connected through to the rear wheel, and the machine is stationary, this represents a fair load on the driven side. Thus, if the engine is running with the clutch fully disengaged and if the clutch is released suddenly so that the plates snap together, the load on the engine will change equally suddenly from nothing to quite a high load. If the engine is running at a low or moderate speed, this sudden load will make it stop dead. If running rapidly to start with, it may be able to pick up the load, but it will be with a sudden jerk. Thus the only *smooth* way to pick up the load is to let the clutch out *gradually*, so that the driving plate can rub and slip against the driven plate while the whole drive is taken up smoothly and the clutch is fully released.

Clutch Control. Letting the clutch pick-up gradually is the only way to get smooth starting from a standstill. When changing gear there is little or no load to take up since the machine is moving and the clutch here is mainly a convenience for getting the gears in and out of mesh without having to bother about synchronizing engine speed. Hence in gear changing the clutch action can be much snappier—virtually "in and out."

Letting the clutch slip unnecessarily is in any case bad, for as we have seen, when the clutch plates are slipping there is rubbing wear on the friction lining. Too much of this and the lining will be worn right down and no longer be effective. Then the clutch will continue to slip, even in the fully engaged position. In an actual clutch there is never *complete* disengagement of the driven discs from the driving discs and so even when it is held in the fully disengaged position there is likely to be some rubbing wear. Hence using the clutch to disengage the engine when running and holding it disengaged from the drive in gear is bad practice, and promotes high clutch wear. It does not matter about the clutch being held disengaged so much with the gearbox in neutral for here the load on the driven side is only the gearbox main gear which can turn freely on the main shaft.

Gearbox Construction. The gearbox is separately detailed in a simplified diagram in Fig. 7. The main gear is in mesh with the pinion gear on the driven side of the clutch, and thus is always driven by the engine when the clutch is engaged (i.e. clutch plates in contact). On the inside is a smaller gear formed integrally with it, and on the other end of the mainshaft there is another smaller gear, also freely fitting on the mainshaft so that it can be rotated independently of the shaft. Separating these two gears is a splined length of shaft on which fits a specially shaped sliding member called a dog, with faces so shaped that if brought up against either gear the dog locks on to the gear. Since the dog is locked on to the shaft as far as rotation is concerned by the splines, engagement of the dog with either gear means that that gear also becomes locked to the shaft and thus turns with the shaft.

Sideways movement of the dog is controlled by a selector fork, free to slide along a spindle. Operation of the gearchange twistgrip to the first

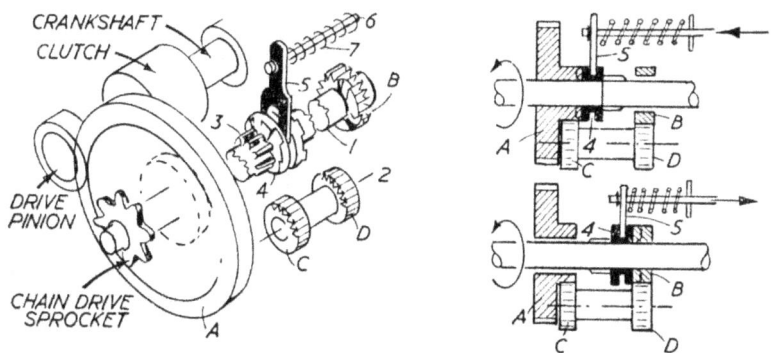

Fig. 7. Simplified Diagrammatic Illustration of the Two-speed Gearbox

The top right-hand sketch shows 2nd gear engaged with the drive between gear A and the mainshaft, gear A locked to the mainshaft (1) by the dog (4). Lower right sketch shows 1st gear position, drive being through gears C and D on layshaft (2) to gear B now locked to mainshaft (1) by dog (4). The dog is moved to the gear selection positions by the selector fork (5) moving on its spindle (6). The spring (7) tends to move the selector to 2nd gear position. In neutral position the dog (4) is in the central position on the mainshaft (1) and thus disengaged from both A and B.

gear position moves the selector one way; and moving the twistgrip to the second gear position moves it to the other extreme—carrying the dog with it in each case and locking either the small gear or the larger (double) gear to the mainshaft. In the neutral position the selector also assumes its mid-position, with the dog in the centre of the splined section of the shaft and thus not contacting either gear.

Changing Gear. Moving the twistgrip to the first gear position, pulls the control cable, which moves the selector in the gearbox against the action of the spring assembled on the spindle with it. It moves to the right-hand side so that the dog is brought up against the smaller inside gear, and so locks this gear to the mainshaft. The drive from the clutch is now transmitted to the gearbox mainshaft via the larger gear. Its smaller pinion on the inside face (still freely rotating independently of the shaft) drives the small layshaft gear assembly which is meshing with the inside gear.

On changing to second gear the selector arm is moved in the opposite direction (to the left) carrying with it the dog to engage the large gear and lock this to the shaft. The drive is now direct from the clutch to this large gear, with the layshaft gears still being driven and also driving the inner gear, although this latter gear is now merely running free on the shaft. It will be appreciated, that the spring on the selector spindle is now helping to maintain second gear by keeping the selector over and holding the dog in mesh with the main driving gear. The actual operation of the gearbox, shown simplified in Fig. 7, can be followed in more precise detail by studying Figs. 44, 45 and 49. The mechanical movements involved are actually quite simple and can be readily understood.

PEDAL SYSTEM

The pedal cranks are mounted on a separate spindle behind the gearbox unit. A simplified drawing is shown in Fig. 8 whilst more precise details are given in Fig. 49, where the complete engineering layout can be studied.

Locking and Disengaging. The pedal cranks are locked to the spindle but the large gear in the middle is free running on this spindle. It comes up against a short length of "quick" thread formed on the spindle and is held in this position by a spacer tube fitted over the other end of the shaft. The gear meshes with the inner gear on the gearbox layshaft and is thus being driven by the engine in both gear positions and neutral, but merely idling on the spindle.

The boss of the gear, facing the threaded length of spindle, is serrated. Mounted on the spindle close by—actually on the thread—is a driver also with serrated faces, held away from the gear boss by a spring. If, however, the pedals are rotated in the direction for normal pedalling the spring is compressed and the driver is forced to run down the threaded portion of spindle so that its serrated face locks against the serrated face on the gear boss. The gear is now locked to the pedal crank spindle as long as the pedals are kept turning fast enough to keep up with the speed of the gear as driven by the engine (if the engine is running); or as long as pressure is kept on the pedals, if the engine is not running.

Thus this simple locking action provides a means of turning over the engine by the pedals for starting; and also, if the engine is running, it is possible to assist it if necessary (e.g. on a steep incline) by pedalling, with the pedal drive automatically disengaging in both cases when pressure on the pedals is released. For starting purposes the engine would be in neutral gear position, but equally it will be seen that the pedals will drive the engine in any gear position selected. In either 1st or 2nd gear position, it will also drive the rear wheel via the gearbox mainshaft, sprocket and chain with the engine not running. This, of course, requires considerable effort since the pedal drive has also to turn the engine over against compression, but if it is necessary to pedal the machine with the engine "dead," disengaging

GENERAL DESCRIPTION AND HANDLING 15

the clutch will disengage the engine from the gearbox and thus the pedal drive is relieved of this extra work. For emergency pedal-driving, in fact, a locking clip is provided on the handlebars to hold the clutch lever fully in.

Back-pedalling Brake. The pedal crank spindle assembly also provides an entirely different action initiated by back-pedalling. A back-pedalling movement throws the driver away from the central gear. It moves it farther to the left along the quick start thread and forces the outer serrated

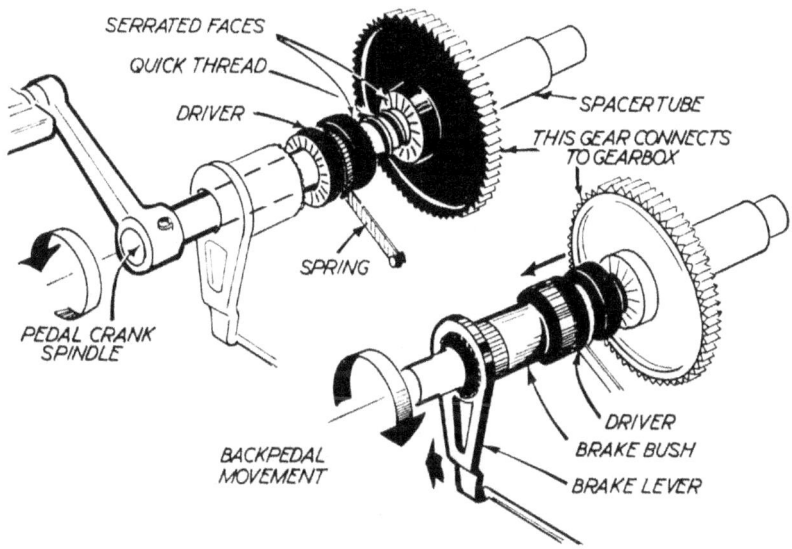

FIG. 8. SIMPLIFIED DRAWING OF THE PEDAL CRANK SPINDLE ASSEMBLY
In the left hand (*top*) sketch the stationary position is shown. Pedalling brings the driver in engagement with the large gear. Back-pedalling (*bottom right*) engages the brake bush with the driver and actuates the brake lever.

face against the serrated face of the brake bush mounted in the crankcase cover. The driver is now locked to this bush. The outer portion of the brake bush is splined and on it is fitted the brake lever, also splined, so that brake lever and brake bush are locked together. Thus, when the driver is locked to the spindle, it is also locked to the brake bush and because it is still on the thread the back-pedalling movement is transmitted directly to the brake lever which is rotated in a similar direction and so pulls the brake rod or brake cable to operate the rear brake. The action is illustrated in simplified form in Fig. 8 and again is quite easy to understand.

Chain Drive. The final drive between the sprocket on the gearbox mainshaft and a similar (but larger) sprocket on the rear wheel hub is by roller chain, identical in this respect to a bicycle chain except that the chain is of sturdier construction. As can be followed, the drive can be either from the engine through one of two selected gears, or by pedals with the engine side of the drive fully disengaged by the clutch, and with the gear change in the second position for a favourable ratio. More detailed descriptions of these various components for the purpose of dismantling, replacement, etc., will be found in Chapter 5, Section 8.

EQUIPMENT

It is no more difficult to ride and handle the Quickly than it is to ride a pedal bicycle. In fact, in some respects it is easier—and certainly far more

FIG. 9. QUICKLY-N MODEL (S IS BASICALLY SIMILAR)

1. Control group (clutch, gearchange, decompressor)
2. Control group (throttle and front brake)
3. Tank for petrol/oil mixture
4. Horn
5. Saddle
6. Luggage carrier
7. Pump
8. Handle for lifting
9. Exhaust silencer

effortless! The main features of the complete machine are shown in Figs. 9 and 10. Details differing from an ordinary pedal bicycle (apart from the engine and tank) are: the toolbox incorporated in the front forks underneath the headlamp and opened by unscrewing the screw at the bottom; the handlebar lock working on the front forks with the key position just above the screw just mentioned; the carrying handle fitted to the right-hand side of the engine and frame, which will be found most useful for lifting the machine up or down steps; the provision of a sprung stand under the engine and an additional side-prop stand on the S and L models;

Fig. 10. Quickly-L Model

1. Handlebars
2. Tank
3. Saddle
4. Panniers (extra equipment)
5. Leg shield
6. Pedal
7. Side-prop stand
8. Central stand

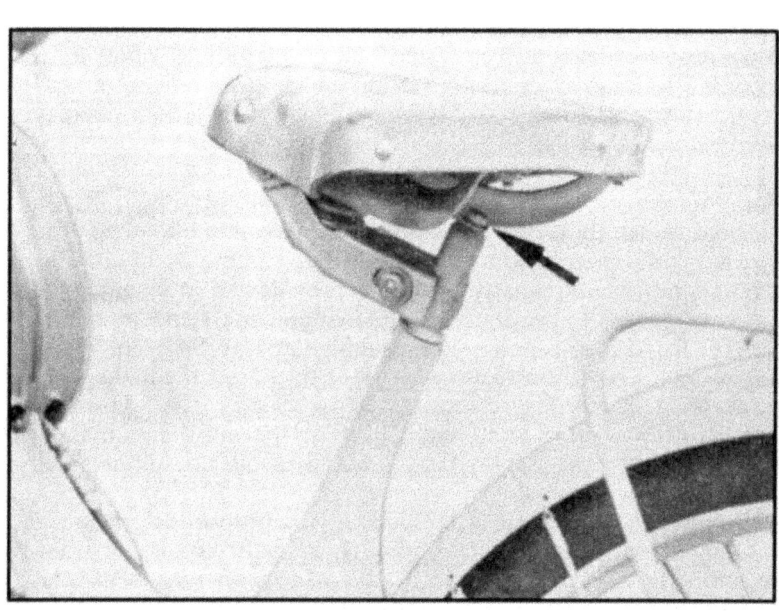

Fig. 11. Saddle Adjustment
This can be made by loosening the bolt marked with an arrow.

and the position of the pump (on the right-hand side of the luggage carrier on the N and S models, and in front of the frame on the L model).

Before attempting to ride the machine for the first time the saddle position should be checked for a comfortable riding position and, if necessary, adjusted. The saddle tube is split at the lower end. The long clamp bolt, with the head visible at the upper end of the saddle tube, has a spreader nut fitted at the bottom. Tightening this bolt draws the nut up the split section of the tube forcing it outwards thus gripping the stem tightly in position (Fig. 11). To adjust the height of the stem it is therefore necessary to slacken off the clamp bolt and, if necessary, drive downwards to relieve the "spread" of the tube. Height can then be adjusted as required, and the clamp bolt tightened right up again. The tube must not be withdrawn higher than the point O marked on it otherwise there will be insufficient length remaining inside the frame for a proper location.

FUEL AND OIL

The engine is designed to run on a petrol-oil mixture. The only lubrication the engine unit receives internally is the oil in this mixture, so that running on plain petrol would ruin the engine in a very short time. All the time the engine is running, therefore, the quantity of lubricant present is proportional to the engine speed and thus automatically adjusted to requirements. With the throttle fully closed a minimum amount of cylinder lubricant is drawn in. This is perfectly satisfactory when the engine is idling but may give marginal lubrication when the throttle is fully closed and the engine is being driven faster than normal idling speed, e.g. when descending a long, steep hill. Hence under such circumstances it is generally advisable to give an occasional burst of throttle to increase the flow of oil to the engine.

Fuel Mixture. The recommended proportion of oil to petrol is 1 to 24, equivalent to one-third of a pint of oil to every gallon of petrol. This is a somewhat lower proportion of oil than that commonly used with two-stroke engines but is entirely adequate provided a good quality oil of the correct grade is always used. The manufacturers specify a relatively heavy oil for the petrol-oil mixture, designated as SAE 40. The SAE rating of oils is based on their viscosity or thickness, the higher the SAE viscosity number the thicker the oil, and vice versa. The SAE number is not necessarily a measure of the *quality* of the oil. Thus it is strictly advisable to insist on using a known brand of oil, as well as specifying the SAE number required.

It should not be necessary to increase the proportion recommended even with a brand new engine, although a small increase will have no effect on performance. The main trouble which can arise from using too high a proportion of thick oil "to be on the safe side" is that it may tend to settle out of the petrol as a separate layer at the bottom of the tank

GENERAL DESCRIPTION AND HANDLING 19

while standing so that the carburettor fills with oil instead of petrol next time and the engine will not start. Too *little* oil in the fuel mixture will result in the engine receiving inadequate lubrication which will increase wear or even lead to parts seizing or becoming permanently damaged and calling for replacement.

Recommended commercial grades of oil include Castrol SAE 40, Energol 40, Essolube 40, Mobiloil 40, Shell SAE 40.

The lower part of the engine, i.e. the gearbox unit, is lubricated by running it immersed in oil, the level of which requires periodic topping-up. Other parts such as the cables, driving chain, etc., are lubricated by oil or grease applied at regular intervals as specified in the Lubrication Table and Lubrication Chart (Chapter 3).

Petrol Grade. Standard grade petrol is perfectly satisfactory for the Quickly and the use of premium fuels is not recommended. Also the extra expense is quite unnecessary. In fact the engine may not run so well on "premium" grades. Tank capacity is 3·1 litres or approximately 5½ pints on early models, and 4·45 litres or a gallon on later models,* of which ¾ pint is retained as a reserve supply until the fuel tap is turned to the "reserve" position. As normal "refill" capacity, therefore, is only 4¾ or 7 pints (depending on the model) it is not always convenient to refill direct at a garage. A better proposition usually is to have a one gallon can for collecting mixture for refilling in which the mixture is made up. It can then be transferred to the tank via a funnel, with the balance normally kept at home.

Reserve Tap. The fuel tap is the same on all models, located at the bottom of the tank on the right-hand side (Figs. 12 and 13). With the handle in the forward position (exposing the letter Z) the tap is switched to the "off" position. In the vertically down position (in line with the pipe) the tap is in the normal "on" position, but leaving a remainder of about ¾ pint of fuel in the tank when run "dry" in this position. By switching the tap to the rearward position (exposing the letter R uppermost), this further ¾ pint can be drawn on as a reserve. Since the average performance of the Quickly is 120–150 miles per gallon (depending on how it is driven), a normal full tank of fuel can be relied upon for about 100–120 miles of driving, with a further safety margin of 15–20 miles given by the reserve capacity of the tank.

The value of having such a reserve is obvious and it should be kept in hand for an emergency, or a warning that a refill is necessary. It is bad practice to get into the habit of switching the tank tap to the reserve position for running with the tank full.

* On the S 23, S/2 23 and F the total fuel tank capacity is approximately 1¾ gallons.

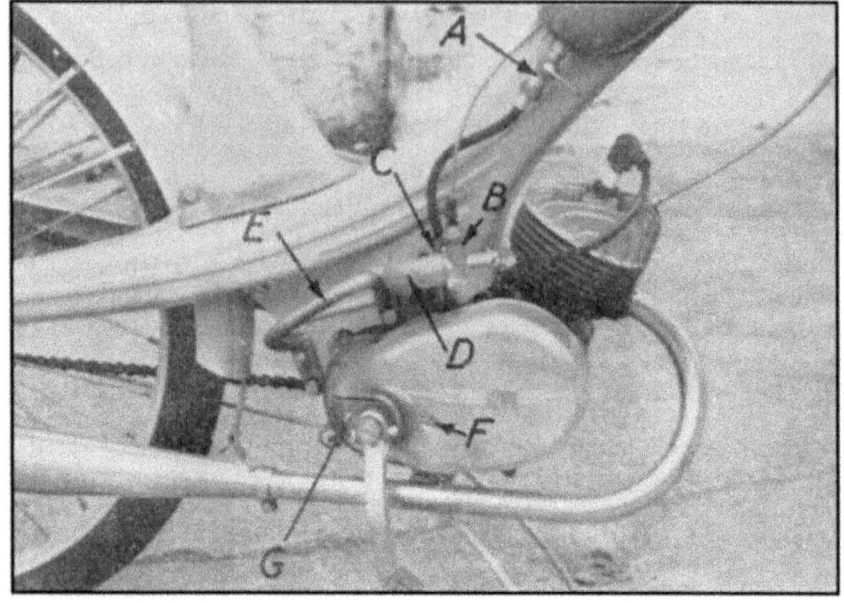

Fig. 12. Details of Quickly-N and -S
A. Fuel tap (off position shown)
B. Carburettor
C. Tickler
D. Rubber elbow connecting to air filter
E. Lifting handle
F. Screw holding cover plate
G. Gearbox oil filler plug

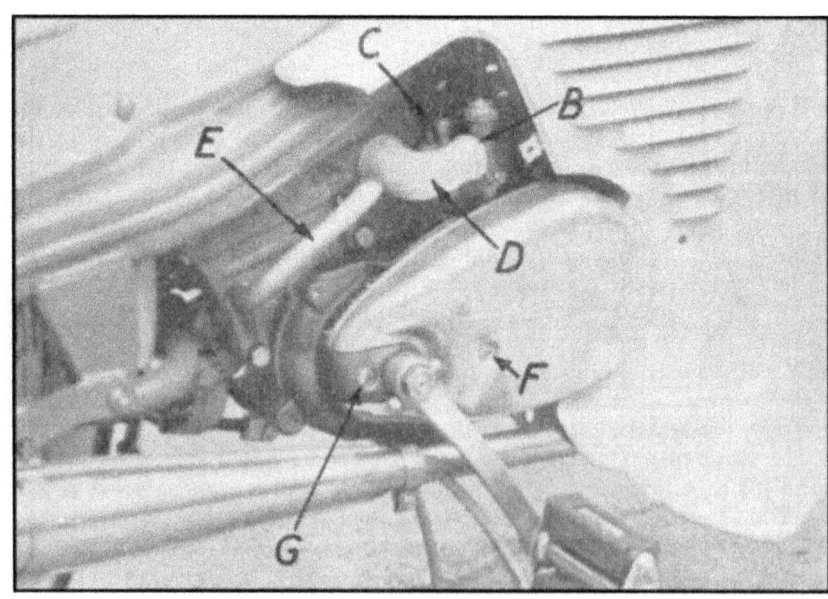

Fig. 13. Details of Quickly-L
Key applies as for Fig 12.

GENERAL DESCRIPTION AND HANDLING 21

Filling the Tank. Failing a garage which dispenses "ready mixed" petrol fuel, it is usually more convenient to buy fuel in gallon cans and refill the tank at home. The correct way to make up a petroil mixture is to turn the petrol tap "off," then add the oil first (to the tank or container) and then pour the petrol on top. Shaking the tank, or turning the container end over end a number of times, will then ensure uniform mixing. Petrol should never be poured first into the tank as it will tend to fill the pipe to the tap and not mix with added oil. Hence the first supply to the carburettor will be pure petrol, which will contain no lubricant when drawn through into the engine. Before refilling a tank from a prepared mixture which has been standing for some time it is always advisable to shake the mixture first.

OPERATING THE ENGINE

Controls. Engine and front brake controls are mounted on the handlebars in identical positions on all models. (*See* Figs. 14 and 15.) The only difference between the N and S and the L machines is the shape of the clutch lock and decompressor lever, and the shape and position of the combined headlamp-dipswitch-horn button.

The other controls used for starting are the "tickler" on top of the carburettor (Figs. 12 and 13) and the choke, the latter being located on the frame at the bottom left-hand side just above the engine crankcase (Fig. 16).

Tickler. The tickler operates directly on the float in the carburettor chamber (*see* Figs. 12 and 40) and when depressed pushes the float down and ensures that the float chamber is quite full of fuel. If the tickler is held down the float chamber will overflow so that excess petrol runs into the carburettor, which will make for difficult starting. Thus the tickler should only be used in moderation when the engine is to be started from cold, and depressed only until the first trace of overflowing fuel appears on top of the carburettor through the small hole in the top—never longer.

Choke. Turning the choke control (Fig. 16) closes a flap over the carburettor air intake which both improves the suction and richens the mixture drawn into the engine (i.e. the mixture consists of a higher proportion of petrol to air). This again is quite drastic in action. The choke is *only* necessary when starting an engine from cold, particularly in cold weather. On later models a semi-automatic choke is fitted. For starting from cold the choke is operated by means of a push-button lever on top of the carburettor. Opening up the throttle once the engine has started and is running then automatically returns the choke control to its original position. One of the main causes of difficult starting with small two-stroke engines is an excessively rich mixture, produced by over-priming the carburettor or over-choking. This results in neat petrol

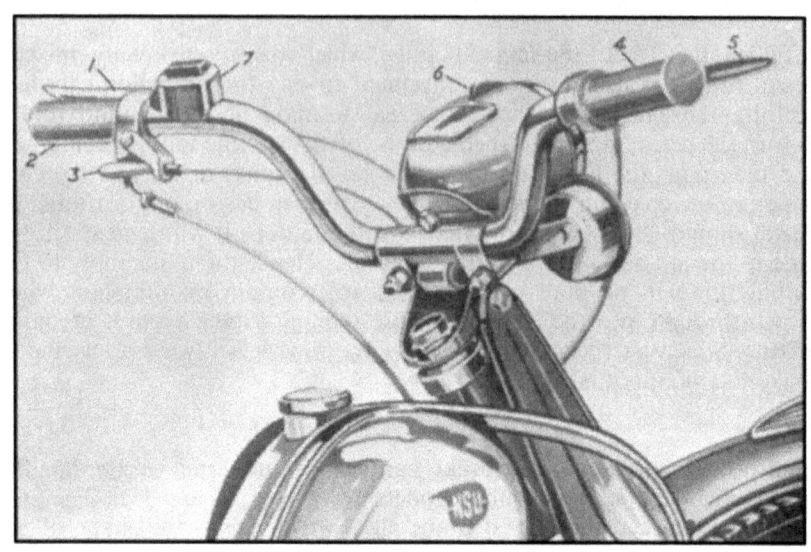

FIG. 14. N AND S MODEL HANDLEBARS

Showing clutch lever (1), gearchange twistgrip (2), decompressor lever (3), throttle twistgrip (4), front brake lever (5) and light switch (6), horn button and dipswitch (7).

FIG. 15. L MODEL HANDLEBARS

Showing clutch lever (1), gearchange twistgrip (2), decompressor lever (3) throttle twistgrip (4), front brake lever (5) and light switch (6). Dipswitch and horn button (normal position) (7).

being drawn into the cylinder and thrown on to the plug, and wetting it so thoroughly that it cannot spark. With a little experience it soon becomes easy to recognize whether an engine will not start because it is too "lean" (not enough petrol, calling for choking), or too "rich" (excessive choking). In the latter case no amount of further turning over of the engine will

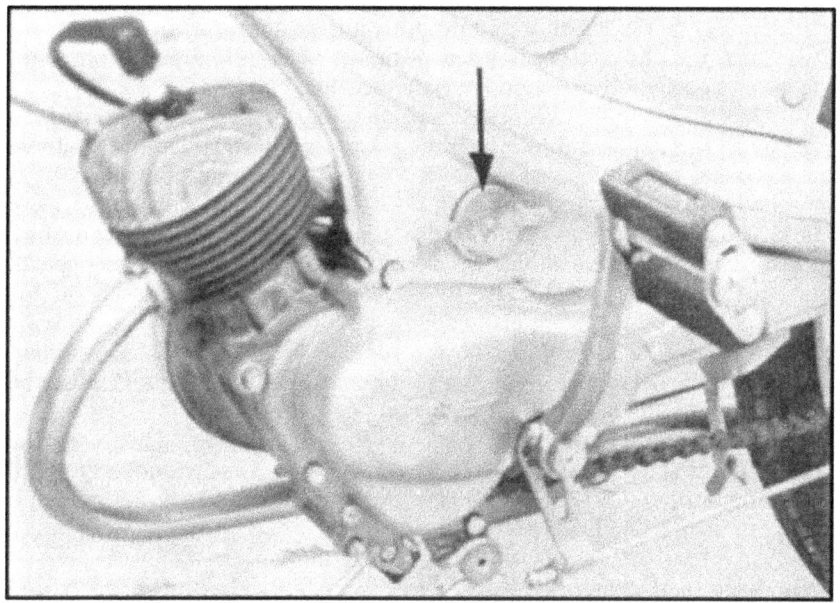

FIG. 16. CHOKE IS OPERATED BY ROTATING CIRCULAR COVER PLATE (ARROWED)

make it start. It will merely make matters worse. The only cure in the case of excessive over-choking is to remove the plug and dry it, open the choke and turn the engine over with the plug still out to help blow out some of the excess fuel, then replace the plug and start again with the throttle set nearly fully open. If the engine is not completely over-choked, opening the choke and turning over with the throttle wide open will often clear it.

Starting-up. For starting, the machine should always be resting on its two wheels, i.e. with the stand (or stands) raised. Make sure that the gearchange twistgrip is in the neutral "*O*" position—if not, pull in the clutch lever and rotate the twistgrip until it is. The pedals provide a "kick-starter" drive, it generally being most convenient to apply pressure to the left pedal, sitting astride the machine, or to the right pedal when standing beside the machine. The appropriate pedal should therefore be turned to a position corresponding approximately to "two o'clock."

Releasing the clutch (i.e. pulling the clutch lever in) will enable the pedals to be turned on their own.

PROCEDURE. Starting procedure is then as follows—
1. Turn the petrol tap to the "on" position.
2. If necessary, work the tickler on the carburettor slowly until there is a slight trace of overflow on top of the carburettor. (In warm weather, just depress the tickler once and do not wait for any overflow.)
3. Turn the choke to the closed position, or operate choke control in the case of semi-automatic choke (late models).
4. Hold the throttle twistgrip about one-quarter to one-third open.
5. With the left thumb, hold the decompressor lever in and push down on the pedal to turn the engine over. The fact that the decompressor is operated will make the engine spin over readily, *but it cannot start when the decompressor valve is open.* Hence it is essential to release the decompressor over about the last third of the swing of the pedal. The engine will normally start almost immediately the decompressor is released on the speed built up by the previous pedalling action.

Once the engine is running the throttle can be closed. The choke flap should also be opened straight away. In cold weather this may cause the engine to stall and stop. Re-start the engine with the choke closed again, then open the flap *partially* and let it run for a little while. Then open the choke completely. Never attempt to drive away with the choke flap still closed or partially closed as this will cause the engine to "flood" and run badly, or stop entirely.

Stopping the Engine. To stop the engine, simply close the throttle and operate the decompressor lever. Starting and stopping is the *only* time the decompressor is used. It will produce an effect at driving speeds. For example, running at near full throttle operating the decompressor lever may be effective in causing the engine to slow down, i.e. the decompressor will work like closing the throttle. But the decompressor should *never be used for this purpose* since it is liable to cause serious damage to the piston. Speed control of the engine should be done *entirely* with the throttle.

DRIVING TECHNIQUE

Driving technique is very simple. Sitting astride the machine with the engine running, pull in the clutch lever as far as it will go and rotate the gearchange twistgrip away from you to the first gear position (1). Then let out the clutch lever gently, at the same time opening the throttle to about one-third to one-half. The reason for letting out the clutch slowly has already been explained. If the engine is allowed to pick up the drive too suddenly the machine will jerk forward, and possibly stop the engine. Very little practice is necessary to get the knack of making smooth starts and once this has been mastered it should become an automatic action, i.e. you do it naturally every time without thinking about it.

GENERAL DESCRIPTION AND HANDLING 25

Clutch Sticking. Sometimes the first start after the machine has been left standing idle for a few days is jerky, not because the clutch has been let out too rapidly but because the clutch plates are partially stuck together with oil. It is most likely to happen in cold weather. If this condition is bad, i.e. the engine stalls as a consequence, it can be cleared by engaging a gear (engine stopped) and pushing the machine forward. Normally, however, no trouble should be experienced from the clutch sticking, unless it requires adjustment or is badly worn. In this instance even full movement of the clutch lever will not disengage the plates completely, either calling for adjustment of the clutch cable (to get more movement at the clutch end), or replacement of the lined clutch discs (badly worn clutch).

Under certain conditions of starting, e.g. starting on a hill, the pedals can be used to assist the engine to get under way. In other words the machine can be pedalled off like a bicycle, at the same time letting in the clutch to engage the engine with first gear.

Choice of Gear. Running in first gear the Quickly will speed up to about 15 m.p.h. on full throttle. This corresponds to an engine speed of about 5,000 r.p.m. The Quickly engine develops maximum power at 5,200 r.p.m. and so it should not be driven faster in that gear. Nor is it good driving to try to make it go faster. The purpose of the second gear is to provide a higher speed ratio between the engine and the back wheel so that the machine can go faster for the same engine speed. Hence having reached about 10 m.p.h. in first gear you should change up into second gear by pulling in the clutch and closing the throttle simultaneously, engaging second gear by rotating the gearchange twistgrip towards you to position 2 and then letting out the clutch again at the same time opening the throttle slightly. Further acceleration can then be achieved by opening up the throttle with second gear engaged.

Second gear is for normal cruising and running; first gear for starting and "pulling" where you want maximum *turning force* applied to the rear wheel. Just as you can ride a bicycle better up a hill if it is fitted with a three-speed so that you can change into "low" and pedal faster, so changing down to first gear on the Quickly on a hill lets the engine run faster to develop more pull. In second gear, under similar conditions, the engine would "labour," lose speed, and the machine would slow up—in the same way that you lose speed trying to ride a bicycle up a hill in high gear.

These points are illustrated in Fig. 17 which shows the engine speeds corresponding to the same road speed in first and second gear. This diagram underlines a basic requirement in changing down. If in second gear the engine is doing approximately 2,000 r.p.m., at the same road speed in first it would be doing approximately 4,000 r.p.m. To change from second down to first gear at the same speed, therefore means that a simultaneous alteration of engine speed from 2,000 to 4,000 r.p.m. is required. In other words after releasing the engine from the drive wheel by pulling in the clutch lever the engine must be speeded up again before it can be re-engaged with the drive in the lower first gear.

Smooth Gear Change. In practice it is not necessary to be exact for the design of the gearbox unit allows considerable latitude. But to change down smoothly it is necessary to *open the throttle* on releasing the clutch with the first gear engaged. Otherwise there will be a sharp jerk as the

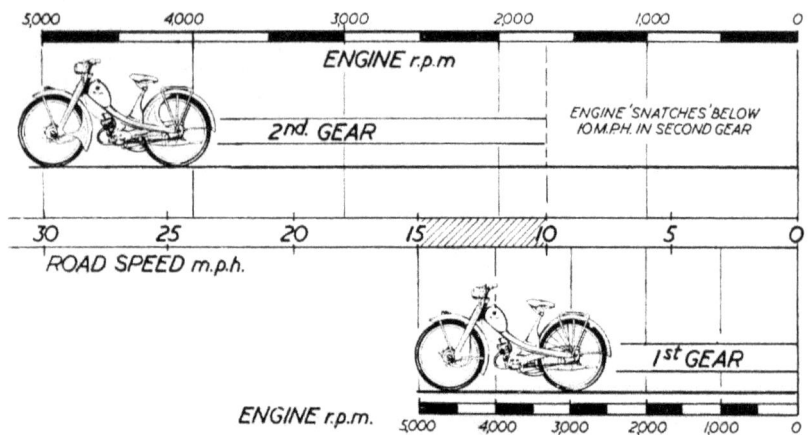

FIG. 17. COMPARISON BETWEEN ENGINE R.P.M. AND ROAD SPEED IN 1ST AND 2ND GEARS (TWO-SPEED MODELS)

drive takes up in the lower gear. This again is a knack readily acquired with a little practice. It is well worth understanding these points and endeavouring to make smooth gear changes always, not only for the satisfaction of good driving technique but also because smooth riding puts less strain on the engine, clutch, gearbox, chain and rear wheel and gives them a longer working life.

Changing-down can also be used as a method of braking or losing speed. The faster your speed in second gear the more you will have to accelerate on letting out the clutch with first gear engaged to change smoothly. Then *closing* the throttle will make the engine act as a brake since, in effect, the rear wheel is trying to drive the engine.

Braking. This, however, does put most of the strain on the chain. For most normal braking requirements the engine will be left in second gear and braking achieved by applying both the front and rear brake together, slowly but firmly. The front brake is worked by the lever on the right-hand handlebar and the rear brake by back-pedalling. On wet or slippery roads, particularly on greasy curves, use the rear brake only for safety. Under all other circumstances use both brakes. Descending a long hill

GENERAL DESCRIPTION AND HANDLING

front and rear brakes can be used alternately to prevent either overheating. Another point to remember in descending a long hill is that with the engine running slowly there may be a tendency for it to become starved of oil, so pull in the clutch occasionally and give the engine a quick burst of throttle to suck in more mixture.

On ascending slopes, or where it has been necessary to slow right down, the engine may begin to labour if left in second gear and so the drive must be changed down to first gear. It is seldom advisable, for instance, to attempt to drive at a speed of below 10 m.p.h. in second gear, or below 15 m.p.h. on a hill without changing down otherwise the engine may tend to "snatch." Also where it is necessary to proceed slowly, such as in traffic, always change down in good time.

Slipping the Clutch. It is very bad practice to "slip the clutch" on short hills, i.e. let out the clutch just enough to make it slip so that the engine runs faster instead of labouring and still continues to drive. You may get over the hill in this way but the resulting wear on the clutch in that short distance achieved may be greater than that for thousands of miles of normal driving. Always change down under such circumstances, if in second gear. If the hill is such a steep one that even in first gear the engine still has to labour hard, the best thing for you to do is to assist the engine by pedalling.

Economy Driving. Other rules for economical driving are: drive in second gear all the while you can (i.e. while you can maintain a speed of 15 m.p.h. or greater); and on the open road cruise at about three-quarters maximum throttle (which will give you minimum fuel consumption). When you have to stop, always return the gear change to neutral (*O*) and let the clutch out. Keeping the machine stationary in gear with the clutch pulled in will result in wear on the clutch plates. At the end of a run, turn off the fuel tap as soon as you have stopped the engine. This will both prevent wastage of fuel and make for easier starting next time since the carburettor cannot become flooded. It is best, in fact, to turn off the fuel tap some two or three hundred yards *before* the end of a run so that this distance is completed on fuel drawn from the carburettor itself. This will leave the curburettor dry so that there is no chance of oil settling out from the fuel inside it and blocking the jet. Alternatively, having come to a standstill at the end of the run, turn off the fuel tap and let the engine run itself dry and stop.

Emergency Pedalling. In an emergency the Quickly can be pedalled like an ordinary bicycle by engaging second gear and holding the clutch lever in and locking it in this position with the small wire catch on the handlebars (*see* Figs. 14 and 15). This will then get you home if you have run out of fuel or the engine will not run and you cannot find the cause on the spot.

With this setting, the pedals are connected to the back wheel via the second gear and the chain and only the "driven" side of the clutch is being turned. There may, however, be some rubbing contact of the clutch plates and so it is not advisable to pedal the machine in this condition for any longer period than is necessary.

Turn the Fuel Tap off! Since the Quickly engine is gravity-fed from the tank the petrol tap should always be turned off when the engine is not running for any appreciable period of time. If this is not done, and the carburettor float is prevented from staying in its proper position—e.g. by the machine being tilted excessively, or dirt preventing the float needle seating properly, fuel can continue to flow down into the crankcase of the engine. This could cause damage to the engine on starting up, and even a bent connecting rod.

3 Regular Maintenance

RUNNING-IN AND LUBRICATION

Running-in. On any new engine components are set up to close fits. Also the finishes obtained from machining operations, etc. do not necessarily correspond to the best "running fits." The latter are established by letting the engine run under its own power and so "bed down" or "run-in" all rubbing surfaces to a highly satisfactory finish. During this period individual high spots are rubbed down and the surfaces polished by friction. Close initial fits are essential for this to occur, which is why a new engine is often said to be stiff, but they also mean that a fair amount of extra heat may be developed in parts of the engine due to this excess friction.

Hence it is never good practice to race a brand new engine, or to let it run for long periods at the same speed. Two-stroke engines are generally more robust than four-stroke engines in this respect and normally like working hard. Thus running-in is far less critical than, say, a car engine. Also the construction of the Quickly engine with aluminium piston and cylinder considerably lessens any risk of seizure due to overheating.

The main thing to remember with a new Quickly engine is not to open the throttle more than about three-quarters for running during the first 200–250 miles. Also it will help the engine run-in properly if you drive at varying speeds, rather than hold a strict throttle setting for cruising. During the period 250–500 miles you can cruise at a faster rate and short bursts of full throttle will do good, not harm.

During the whole of this period—up to 500 miles—never let the engine "labour," especially climbing hills. Then, provided you have followed these simple rules the engine should be completely run-in and bedded down at about the 500 mile mark and will run consistently at any speed you want. Its life will be greatly improved if you change the gearbox oil completely at this stage since the original oil may contain metal particles ground off during the running-in period which, if re-circulated with the oil, can cause harm. This is covered in the Lubrication Chart (page 37). Other parts require inspection and attention, if necessary, at this stage—particularly the engine mounting bolts (*see* Inspection Chart, page 38).

Lubrication. Lubrication points are shown in Fig. 18, which also indicates which points are lubricated by grease gun, oilcan, etc. The engine unit has an oil reservoir (gearbox unit) which has three removable plugs, the one at the rear and on the right-hand side being the filler plug (through which oil is added); the one at the front, bottom left is the check plug and the one behind it and slightly lower is the drain plug. Oil recommended for the gearbox is SAE 30 for summer and SAE 20 for winter. Actually an SAE 30 oil would be satisfactory all the year round but since a complete oil change in the gearbox is recommended every two–three

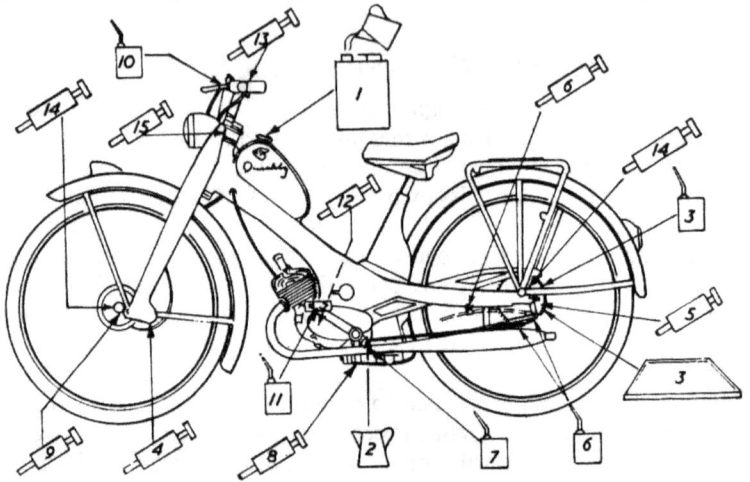

FIG. 18. LUBRICATION CHART (NUMBERS REFER TO POINTS LISTED IN LUBRICATION TABLE)
Note that points 2 and 12 are reached from the right-hand side of the machine.

months there is some advantage in changing the grade, say, in October and April. An SAE 80 gear oil is also suitable for all-the-year round use.

On a new engine the gearbox oil should *invariably* be changed, flushed out and refilled with fresh oil after the running-in period (500 miles). The meticulous owner would carry out this operation twice—the first time at about 300 miles on a new engine, and then again after 600 miles. Subsequently the manufacturers recommend changing the oil every 1,200 miles, although changing it at three-monthly intervals is probably more satisfactory if the monthly mileage does not greatly exceed 500 miles.

The gearbox oil should always be changed when the engine is warm, i.e. after the engine has been run for some time. A tin or suitable receptacle with a capacity of at least ¼ pint should be placed under the drain plug position and the drain and filler plugs removed by unscrewing, using a screwdriver to start them, then unscrewing with the fingers. Oil in the box will then drain off into the can. This old oil is of no further use and should be thrown away.

REGULAR MAINTENANCE 31

Flushing is always advisable before refilling with new oil, although many people do not consider it necessary. The object of using a flushing oil is simply to remove any solid or semi-solid particles, etc., remaining in the gearbox which have not drained out with the old oil. The gearbox should *always* be flushed when changing the oil after the running-in period, and *at least* once a year thereafter at an appropriate oil change. Flushing at every oil change will ensure maximum protection and long engine life.

To flush the gearbox, the drain plug is replaced when all the old oil has drained out, the check plug removed and flushing oil added until it begins to spill out of the check plug hole. Replace check plug and filler plug and start and run the engine for a minute or so to circulate the flushing oil. Then remove all three plugs and let the flushing oil drain off completely. This also is waste oil, to be thrown away.

Finally, replace the drain plug, making sure that it is done up tightly. Fill with new engine oil of the recommended grade until it just begins to flow out of the check plug hole and finally replace check and filler plugs tightly.

The driving chain should receive frequent lubrication with an oilcan filled with ordinary light machine oil, applying the oil quite generously to the rollers. The chain should never be allowed to run dry as this will greatly increase the rate of wear.

Since the chain is exposed and operated in an oily state it will tend to pick up grit and dirt, so fairly frequent cleaning is recommended. The manufacturers specify that this should be done every 600 miles, so make it a regular monthly or three-monthly job, depending on your mileage.

To remove the chain, first rotate the pedals until the spring link is in a convenient position and spring the clip holding this link off with a screwdriver (Fig. 19). The other part of the link can then be withdrawn and the chain "broken" so that it can be taken off. Drop the chain in a tin of petrol or paraffin and, using a stiff brush, clean each link thoroughly of all dirt and grit. Follow by swilling the whole length of chain through the petrol (or paraffin) and lay on a clean surface, such as old newspaper.

To re-grease the chain, chain grease should be put in a tin and heated until it is quite liquid. Then, holding each end of the chain, run it through the liquid grease until each link has received a generous coating (including the end links being held). Hold the chain by one end and let it hang so that surplus grease drips off. Then replace the chain in position on the machine making sure that the spring link is assembled the *right way round*, i.e. with the open end pointing *away* from the direction of travel of the chain. (*See* Fig. 20.)

Other details of lubrication are covered under the separate maintenance headings which follow.

Maintenance after Running-in Period on New Engines. Gearbox oil should be drained, the gearbox flushed and refilled with new oil at the conclusion of the first 500 miles; or at 300 miles and 600 miles, if preferred.

Fig. 19. Details of Chain on Rear Sprocket
A. Chain tension adjuster (one each side)
B. Spring link on chain

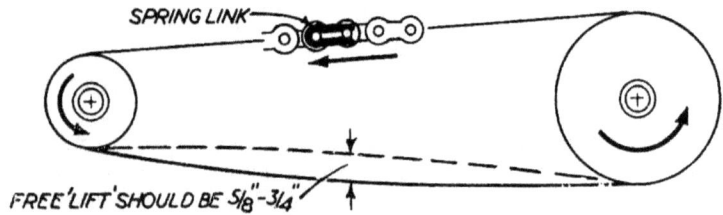

Fig. 20. Chain Tension
Correct chain tension is determined by the amount of "sag" illustrated. Note that the spring link must always come on the outside of the chain, fitted the way round shown.

The engine mounting bolts should be checked and re-tightened if they show the slightest signs of having slackened off.

ROUTINE MAINTENANCE

Regular Weekly Maintenance. The tyre pressures should be checked weekly. Tyres should be pumped up hard so that it is just possible to press in with the thumb. The inner tube valve is of the bicycle type and will not work a conventional tyre pressure gauge used for motor-cars.

The rollers of the driving chain should be oiled.

REGULAR MAINTENANCE

Check the cable-clamping bolts on the headlamp and tail lamp and re-tighten them if necessary.

IN WINTER OR DIRTY WEATHER

1. Using high-pressure grease in the grease gun, lubricate—grease nipples on the front fork swinging link bearings (Lubrication Chart, point 4).
2. Quickly-L only—add grease to the nipples on either side of the rear-wheel swinging arm until excess grease is seen coming out of the bearing (Lubrication Chart, point 5).
3. Quickly-L only—apply grease to nipple on rear brake Bowden cable until grease is seen emerging from each end of the cable sheathing (Lubrication Chart, point 6).
4. Clean the machine, using water and a soft cloth or washleather on the frame and enamelled areas. The outside of the engine can be cleaned with paraffin or petrol. Chrome parts can be cleaned with soapy water, or if very dirty with a proprietary chrome cleaner. Enamelled surfaces can be polished with a car-type polish.

Regular Monthly Maintenance

1. Check the level of the oil in the gearbox by removing the filler and check plugs and adding oil to bring up to the level of the check plug, if necessary. Always use only the specified grade of oil for topping-up the gearbox.
2. Quickly-N and Quickly-S—grease both ends of the back brake rod (Lubrication Chart, point 7) and the centre stand pivots (Lubrication Chart, point 8).
3. Quickly-S—grease side stand pivot.
4. Check the chain tension and, if necessary adjust. (*See* Chapter 5, Section 5.)
5. Remove the spark plug and check its condition. (*See* Chapter 6) Check the gap between the electrodes on the spark plug. (*See* Fig. 21.) This should be 0·020 in., which can be checked against a feeler gauge. Alternatively, use a doubled-over thickness of cigarette packet, which is about this thickness. If necessary to open the gap, the side electrode can be prised out carefully with a small screwdriver or a knife blade. To close the gap, tap the side electrode gently with a small spanner or similar tool. It is more usual for the gap to "grow" and require closing down periodically than it is for it to close up. If the points are dirty they should be thoroughly cleaned by scrubbing with a small wire brush, checking the gap again after this operation.

IN SUMMER. The greasing points dealt with under "weekly maintenance" can be left to monthly intervals. Also cleaning of the machine and engine.

IN WINTER. The driving chain should be removed, thoroughly cleaned and regreased before replacing.

Regular Three-monthly Maintenance

1. Drain gearbox and refill with new oil to correct specification.
2. Disconnect all Bowden cables, in turn, and drip oil into the upper ends until it runs out at the lower end of the sheathing. Grease each end of the cable where it works in the sheathing. To reach the lower end of the clutch cable it will be necessary to remove the left-hand engine cover plate.
3. Grease the speedometer drive (Lubrication Chart, point 9).

Fig. 21. The Spark Plug
This is readily removed for inspection, cleaning and adjustment. Gap between electrodes should be 0·020 in. Check at regular intervals.

4. Oil hand-lever pivots with light machine oil (Lubrication Chart, point 10).
5. Oil pedal bearings by laying the machine over to one side, dripping on oil and rotating the pedals (Lubrication Chart, point 11).
6. Remove the right-hand engine cover plate, also the flywheel (*see* Chapter V, Section 8) and apply a layer of bearing grease to the lubrication pad for the magneto-drive shaft (*see* Lubrication Chart, point 12).
7. Remove the air filter from the carburettor (*see* Chapter 5, Section 6) and take apart. The filter pad should be cleaned thoroughly in petrol and then preferably dried off by blowing with the tyre pump (or a compressed air line at the local garage). Before replacing, dip the pad in light oil and allow to drain until no more drips form.

8. Check all screws and bolts for tightness, particularly the engine mounting bolts, engine head nuts, etc. Also the silencer mounting, and fastenings for accessories.

9. The performance of the engine will probably be improved by decarbonizing the silencer at this point. (*See* Chapter 5, Section 10, for details.)

IN SUMMER. Cleaning and re-greasing of the drive chain can be delayed until this interval.

FIG. 22. THE FLYWHEEL

Contact-breaker points are readily accessible once right-hand cover plate is removed. Rotate flywheel by hand to expose contact breaker under flywheel cut-out.

Six-monthly Maintenance

1. Remove, clean and grease throttle and gearchange twistgrip controls (Lubrication Chart, point 13).

2. Dismantling, cleaning and repacking with fresh grease is advisable for the front and rear wheel bearings (Lubrication Chart, point 14 and *see* Chapter 5, Section 3).

3. Adjust steering head, if necessary, cleaning and replacing grease (Lubrication Chart, point 15. *See* Chapter 5, Section 4.)

4. Decarbonizing of the engine may be advisable at this stage, depending largely on the mileage covered and how the machine has been driven. (*See* Chapter 5, Section 8 and Section 10 for complete details of this operation.)

5. Re-grind the decompression valve in its seat—usually done when decarbonizing. (*See* Chapter 5, Section 10.)
6. All electrical leads should be checked. The state of the contact-breaker points should be examined and the gap adjusted, if necessary. (*See* Chapter 5, Section 7, and Fig. 22.)

TYRE CHANGES

Removal of the front or rear wheel is detailed in Chapter V, Section 3. This is usually the most convenient preliminary move in dealing with a punctured tube. The wheel can then be laid flat on the ground and the outer cover removed with tyre levers, as in the case of an ordinary bicycle.

To remove a tyre the inner tube must be completely deflated. Press the wall of the tyre right in as far as it will go at one side then raise the diametrically-opposite part of the wall sufficiently for it to be prised (with tyre levers) or merely lifted by hand over the rim, when it is a simple matter to pull out the remainder of the tyre wall and so gain access to the inner tube. Replacing the tube and tyre follows the same procedure in reverse. The real art of doing the job is "knack"—not brute force. Excess force must be avoided at all costs as otherwise damage may be done to the rim (using heavy levers), or to the cords of the tyre. In the latter case the tyre is no longer serviceable.

LUBRICATION TABLE

For convenience of reference, items needing attention are grouped under logical period headings. Where alternative headings are shown, e.g. monthly or 1,000 miles, the *shortest* interval should be taken as applying. It should also be appreciated that the longer period check items are in addition to any regular short-period items scheduled for attention at that same time. For example, at the "monthly" period the "weekly" items are also included for attention, and so on.

Once again it can be emphasized that regular and adequate lubrication is probably the most important feature of maintenance; the life of the machine—certainly the life of vital components—is directly related to the degree of regular attention it receives. A film of lubricant over working surfaces not only reduces friction and makes for easier movement, but also provides a degree of protection against corrosion. Rust, once started, is progressive and eats into the surface of ferrous metals so that, even if subsequently cleaned, the surface is no longer smooth. A rust coating, too, expands as it grows, which is why rust causes nuts to "seize" on bolts, etc. It is equally important to keep the machine parts as clean as possible. Grit and similar particles adhering to an oily surface can form an abrasive mixture—promoting a high rate of wear on, for example, the chain if this component is given little or no attention.

REGULAR MAINTENANCE

When	Ref.	Part(s) to be Lubricated	Lubricant (and Remarks)
Weekly	1	Engine	Continuously lubricated by oil mixed with petrol in the tank.
	3	Chain	Oil rollers.*
	4	Front fork swinging links	High-pressure grease
	6	Bowden cable rear brake (model L)	Light machine oil.*
	5	Swinging link, rear suspension (model L)	High-pressure grease.
Monthly or 1,000 Miles	2	Gearbox	Check level and refill, as necessary.
	7	Brake rod ends (models N and S)	Light machine oil.*
	8	Centre stand and side stand	Clean bearings and smear with grease.
	3	Chain (in winter)	Clean and re-grease with chain grease.
	10	Bowden cable ends	Release and oil ends with light machine oil.*
Three-monthly or 3,000 Miles	2	Gearbox	Drain and refill (SAE 20/30 oil).
	10	Bowden cables	Disconnect and grease ends (or use Bowden cable lubricator).
	9	Speedometer drive	High-pressure grease.
	11	Pedal bearings	Light oil.*
	12	Contact-breaker cam	Apply bearing grease or high-pressure grease to felt pad.
	10	Control lever pivots	Oil with light machine oil.*
	3	Chain (summer)	Remove, clean and re-grease with chain grease.
Six-monthly or 5,000 Miles	13	Twistgrips	Clean and smear with high-pressure grease.
	14	Wheel bearings	Clean and re-pack with high-pressure grease.
	15	Steering head	Clean and re-pack with high-pressure grease.

* SAE 20 engine oil is a satisfactory light oil for general lubrication.

INSPECTION TABLE

When	Routine Check and Action
Weekly	Check tyre pressures. Check brakes—adjust cables as necessary. Check cable clamping bolts on headlamp and rear lamp—tighten as necessary. Check engine-mounting bolts (this is important!).
Monthly	Check chain tension—adjust as necessary. The chain sag should be approximately $\frac{3}{4}$ in. (machine unloaded, standing on its wheels, gear in neutral). Remove and clean sparking plug. Check electrode gap and adjust as necessary.
Every Two Months	Adjust clutch cable as necessary—play in the cable should be 2–3 mm. Adjust gearchange cable tension, if necessary. Check engine-mounting bolts, nuts on cylinder head and all other screwed fastenings for tightness. Tighten up where necessary.
Every Three Months	Check play in steering head and take up, if necessary. Check all electrical wiring and connexions. Check contact-breaker gap—should be 0·008 to 0·012 in. Decarbonizing of the cylinder, cylinder head and silencer is also to be recommended at this stage, or after every 1,500 miles.

4 Fault Finding

MANY apparent faults can be due to inexperience, or mishandling, whilst others may develop through neglect. Regular maintenance along the lines covered in the previous chapter will minimize the chance of faults developing. Another important point is always to use recommended lubricants, particularly in the case of the oil mixed with the petrol.

The following table is intended as a general guide for "trouble shooting." Faults of a minor nature can readily be cured with a little common-sense application. More serious faults may require professional attention at a local service station. Even then, however, most of the work involved is well within the capabilities of the average owner who takes the trouble to find out how his (or her) machine works. The chapter on detailed maintenance will be particularly helpful in this respect.

Symptom	Possible Cause	Remedy or Check
Engine will not start	1. Lack of petrol	Check that petrol tap is turned to "on" position ("reserve," if little fuel in tank). Check that there is fuel in tank. Check that choke is operated in starting from cold. Carburettor may be blocked with oil separated out on standing. Carburettor jet may be clogged (clean with bristle).
	2. Too much petrol (strong smell of petrol at carburettor)	Flooding caused by excessive choking, or excessive use of tickler. Try opening throttle right up for starting. If badly flooded it may be necessary to remove and dry plug. Turn engine over with fuel tap off and plug out to clear (choke open, not shut).
	3. No spark	Plug wet through excessive choking (*see above*). Plug fouled up (wants cleaning). Plug electrode gap wrong (check that it is not too large, or too small). Plug lead disconnected. Magneto coil faulty (rare).
	4. Wrong technique	Throttle not opened $\frac{1}{4}-\frac{1}{2}$ position. Decompressor not released in time.
Engine starts, then stops		
1. Almost at once	Too lean	Choke not closed, or should be left partially closed until engine has warmed up.
2. After a short run	Too rich	Choke left open (smell of petrol around carburettor).
3. After a fair run	No fuel	Petrol tap in "off" position. No more fuel in tank.

Table contd.—

Symptom	Possible Cause	Remedy or Check
4. Suddenly, after running normally	No fuel	Check as above.
	Spark plug fouled	Plug may have "whiskered" up—remove and clean.
	No spark	Lead disconnected.
Engine will not stop	1. Decompressor fault	Decompressor valve not opening (cable seized or broken).
	2. Engine carboned up	Engine requires decarbonizing (only likely after a relatively long life without previous attention).
Engine runs badly	*Note:* two-strokes will not "idle" perfectly smoothly like a car engine, so do not confuse a natural roughness with definite faulty running	
Idling	1. Mixture too lean	Air leak on carburettor.
		Air filter blocked (dirty).
		Vent in petrol filler cap blocked.
		Check carburettor adjustment.
	2. Mixture too rich	Choke left closed or partially closed.
		Carburettor jet enlarged.
		Carburettor float stuck or punctured.
		Check carburettor adjustment.
	3. Indeterminate	Plug fouled.
		Contact-breaker points dirty or gap incorrect.
		Spark plug gap incorrect.
		Cylinder head loose.
		Check carburettor adjustment.
Under load	1. Poor carburation	Check carburettor, and as above for "too lean" and "too rich."
	2. Poor ignition	Check condition of plug.
		Check contact-breaker gap and condition of points.
	3. Mechanical	Decompressor valve not seating properly (seat may need re-grinding).
		Cylinder head nuts loose.
		Engine-mounting bolts loose.
Engine lacks pulling power	1. Wrong mixture	Choke left closed.
		Check carburettor adjustment and condition.
	2. Poor ignition	Check as above.
	3. Incorrect timing (retarded)	Check timing. (*See* Chap. V, Section 7.)
	4. Engine or silencer carboned-up	Decarbonize silencer.
		Decarbonize cylinder head and piston.
	5. Unintentional back-pedalling whilst riding	This applies the back brake.
Unusual engine noise		Try to trace the region from which the noise is coming. A different noise from normal engine noise is usually a sign of trouble, or of something loose.
1. Engine very loud	Silencer "blown" or baffle broken	Replace silencer.
2. Rattling noise	Probably something loose, e.g. silencer fastening, engine mounting bolts, accessory clips, etc. May simply be loose tools in tool box	Check that wheels are not loose.
		Check chain sag.
		Check that engine-holding bolts are tight.
3. Engine "knocks"	Incorrect timing	Spark too far advanced. (*See* Chapter V Section 7.)
4. Engine "whines"	Wear or excessive clearance on engine gears or gearbox	Strip and check.
5. Squeaks	Lack of lubrication	Grease suspension grease nipples.
Clutch trouble	1. Does not disengage	Cable requires adjustment.
		Cable seized (lack of lubrication).
		Cable broken.

Table contd.—

Symptom	Possible Cause	Remedy or Check
Brake trouble	2. Slips when in gear 1. Brakes poor 2. One brake more effective than the other 3. Brakes stiff to operate 4. Brakes snatch	Clutch plates stuck (oily). Cable adjusted too tightly. Clutch plates worn. Clutch spring broken. Cable partially seized. Need adjustment. Oil or grease on linings (clean with petrol). Need new linings (no further adjustment available). The front brake will seem more effective for stopping on dry surfaces, and more drastic in action on wet surfaces. A poor performance on one brake usually means that this brake is used most and consequently receives the most wear, requiring more frequent adjustment and earlier replacement of lining. The correct method of braking is to apply both brakes equally (except on treacherous surfaces where the rear brake only should be used). Cable partially seized through lack of lubrication. Linings worn right down, and adjusted "tightly." Replace linings and readjust.
Throttle control trouble	1. Stiff to operate 2. Too loose	Cable partially seized due to lack of lubrication. Friction bolt on twistgrip body too tight. Tighten friction bolt on twistgrip body.
Gearchange trouble	1. Does not select gears properly 2. Stiff to operate	Cable stretched and requiring readjustment. (*See* Chapter V, Section 1.) Wear in gearbox. Cable partially seized due to lack of lubrication.
No lights (engine running)	1. Disconnexion 2. Broken bulb 3. Wiring fault 4. Switch faulty 5. No current from lighting coil	Check for broken wires. Check and replace if necessary. (It is a good idea to carry spare bulbs in the tool kit when night driving.) Bared wires touching frame. Tape up with insulating tape or renew. Contact arm broken or bent. Faulty lighting coil or broken connexion on backplate.
Poor lights	1. Wrong bulbs 2. Partial earth 3. Weak generator	Check bulb voltage and rating. Check wiring for frayed portions which may be touching frame. Faulty lighting coil, or weak flywheel magnets
No horn	1. No connexion 2. Weak generator	Broken wire or switch Faulty lighting coil.
Steering poor	1. Buckled wheel 2. Wheel loose 3. Wheel mis-aligned 4. Frame buckled 5. Tyre pressures very low 6. Steering head bearings loose	Check by rotating. Check. Check. This damage is only likely to result from a crash. A replacement frame will be necessary. Pump up hard—check for slow puncture; check valve for leak. Readjust and tighten.
High fuel consumption	1. Wrong mixture 2. Faulty driving technique	Mixture too rich—check carburation. Choke partially closed. Very dirty air filter. Cruising at full throttle instead of three-quarter throttle. Excessive amount of first-gear driving.

5 Detailed Maintenance

1. CABLES AND CONTROLS

THE best safeguard against control cables sticking or seizing in their sleeving is adequate and regular lubrication. With the exception of the clutch end, all cable ends are readily accessible and should be disconnected and freely oiled about every one-thousand miles. It is also an advantage to grease the ends of the cables lightly where they enter the sheathing, or use a special Bowden cable lubricator for this job (available from most motor accessories shops). The clutch end of the clutch cable can be reached for the purpose of lubricating simply by removing the left-hand engine cover plate.

Adjustment of all cables is quite straightforward. First unscrew the locknut and then adjust the length of the cable by tightening (or unscrewing) the adjusting nut until the desired degree of adjustment has been achieved. (*See* Figs. 37 and 38.) The locknut is then tightened up again strongly to hold this setting. Check the operation of the control again to make sure that this has not altered with the tightening up of the locknut.

In the case of the front brake cable, adjust until the front wheel just spins freely without binding but the brake is brought into operation with a reasonably small movement of the brake lever. The rear brake is adjusted in a similar manner at the cable end on the L model. In the case of the models N and S the rear brake is rod-operated and adjustment is made at the pedal end of the rod (i.e. where it fits in the brake lever arm). The principle of adjustment is exactly the same, shortening the length of rod by means of the adjuster nut (with locknut free) to take up the brake, and vice versa. Where no further adjustment can give effective braking but the visible action is obviously satisfactory, then the brake linings require renewing. (*See* Section 2.) In the case of the model L, apparent premature wear of the rear brake linings may in fact be due to adjustments having led to the brake lever and Bowden cable being no longer roughly at right-angles to each other, so that much of the effective pull is lost. This can be readjusted by slackening off the hexagon nut locking the brake lever in place, pulling the lever off and rotating one or two notches (teeth) to realign them properly.

Adjustment of the clutch cable is necessary as soon as the clutch shows signs of slipping, or failing to disengage properly. The correct amount of play in the clutch cable is about $\frac{1}{10}$ in. (2–3 mm). Adjustment is made

DETAILED MAINTENANCE 43

at the handlebar end in exactly the same manner as with the front brake cable.

The gearchange cable is a little more tricky to adjust since it has to be done by feel. The twistgrip is rotated towards first gear until the dogs in the gearbox are just felt to be engaging. This position is then marked on the grip and a similar position found, and marked, for the beginning of engagement of second gear. The mid-point between these marks is then the correct position of the grip for neutral. Adjustment of cable tension is then made so that this mid-position corresponds to the correct neutral position of the twistgrip, relative to the handlebar mark.

The throttle cable length is adjusted so that when the throttle twistgrip is fully closed the engine continues to tick-over. This is done at the carburettor end, the adjuster being exposed by sliding back the roller sleeve. (*See* Figs. 23 and 24.) The twistgrip should stay in any position to which it is rotated, return movement under spring action being opposed by friction governed by the bolt shown in Fig. 24. Tightening up this bolt will improve the "self-locking" action of the twistgrip.

The decompression control cable should have only a fraction of end play (about 1 mm); adjustable at the handlebar lever in the case of the N and S, and at the point where the cable emerges from the shroud immediately under the headlamp fairing in the case of the model L.

Front brake cables are readily removed, when necessary, by disengaging them at both ends, opening the clip inside the front fork, holding the sheath, and then withdrawing the cable downwards through the handlebar shroud. New cable should be fed back in the reverse direction. The rear brake cable (L model) is released by disengaging the nipple from the brake arm, unscrewing the adjuster out of its bracket and then releasing it from the pedal lever end.

When renewing a clutch cable, remove the chain guard and push the clutch lever in to remove the cable nipple. The front end is released from the handlebar lever. Then a 5-6 ft length of thin wire should be joined to the lower end of the cable by twisting it round the nipple and pulling it through as the cable is withdrawn from the handlebar end. The lower nipple of the new cable is then attached to this wire and pulled back through.

A similar technique is employed when replacing a gearchange cable. To release the cable from the twistgrip end the decompression cable should be released from the decompressor valve (*see* later), the twistgrip released by unscrewing the locking screw (*see* Figs. 25 and 26) and slide outwards off the handlebars. The rubber sleeve on the grip can then be prised up carefully to release the nipple. The bottom end is released by removing the right-hand engine cover and disconnecting from the gearchange lever. A length of thin wire is then attached to the lower nipple and the cable withdrawn upwards from the handlebar end. The lower nipple of the new cable is then attached to the wire and drawn back downwards into position. It is particularly important to ensure on reassembly that the nipple is properly engaged in the twistgrip.

When changing a throttle cable, unscrew the adjuster locknut (carburettor end) and then screw the adjuster right home. Unscrew the top

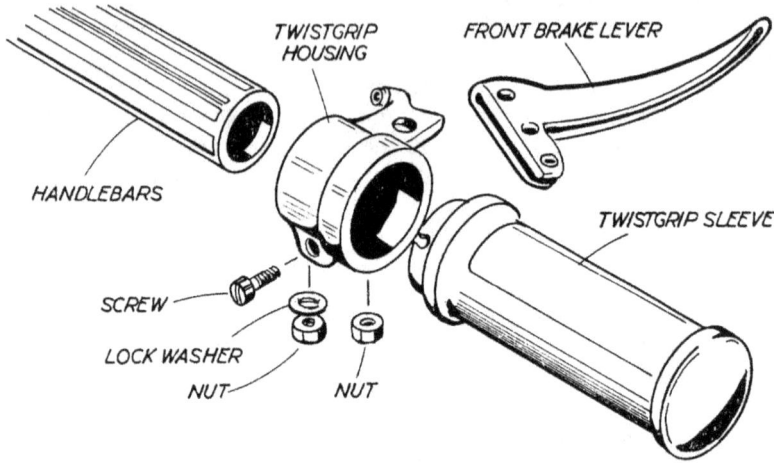

FIG. 23. THROTTLE TWISTGRIP ASSEMBLY ON N AND S MODELS

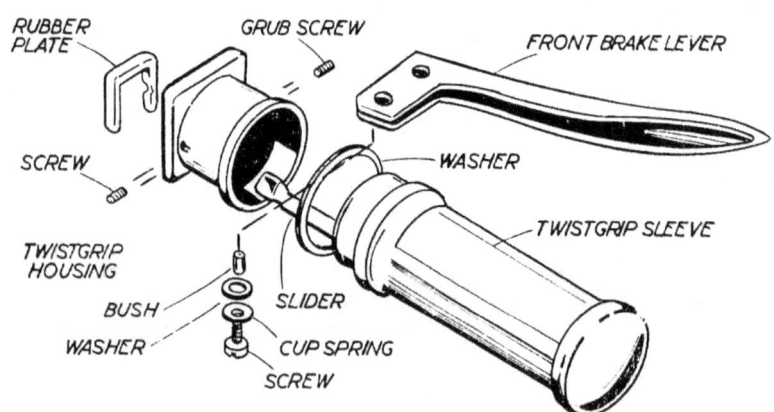

FIG. 24. THROTTLE TWISTGRIP ASSEMBLY ON L MODEL

of the carburettor and remove together with the throttle slide attached to the cable. Release the cable from the slide and set the carburettor parts down on a clean surface. The throttle twistgrip should then be removed completely from the handlebars by unscrewing the holding screw (*see* Figs. 23 and 24) and sliding it off the handlebars, when the cable can be released. To assist in easy withdrawal of the cable and to replace it with

DETAILED MAINTENANCE 45

a new length, it will be found necessary on some models to slacken off the strap holding the fuel tank in place to take pressure off the rubber blocks acting as a cable clamp.

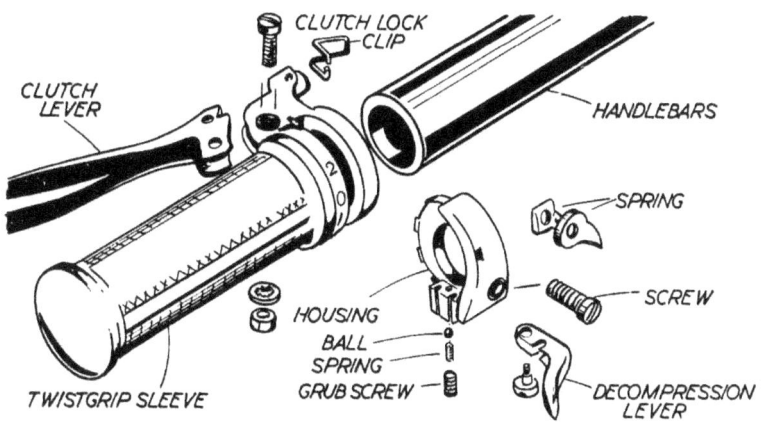

Fig. 25. Gearchange Twistgrip on N and S Models
The S/2 model is basically similar.

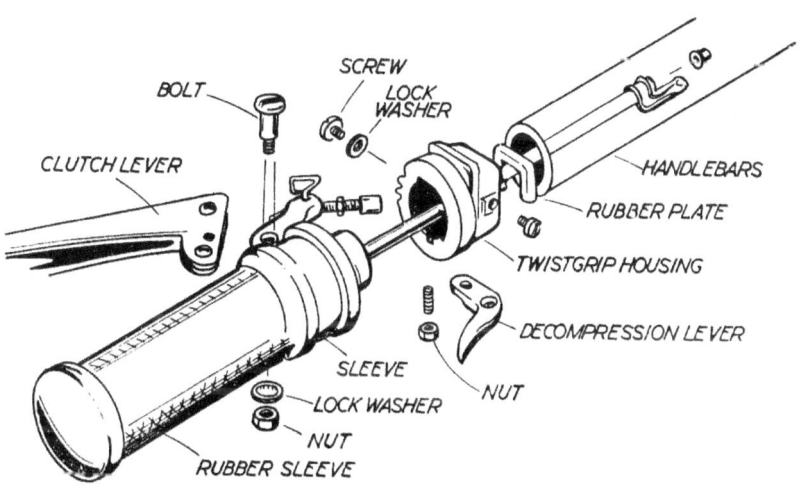

Fig. 26. Gearchange Twistgrip on L Model

The decompression cable is released from the valve end by first pressing down the valve with a screwdriver or similar tool, and then disengaging the cable. The upper end of this cable has a solderless nipple locked with a small screw which if released will enable the cable to be withdrawn. In fitting a new cable the solderless nipple is first attached to the cable tightly, allowing about $\frac{3}{8}$ in. of cable to protrude (Fig. 27). Pass the lower end of the cable down through the sheath when the lower nipple can be engaged properly by pressing it in place with a screwdriver.

Brake and clutch levers are removed by first detaching the cables, then unscrewing the nuts, and withdrawing the pivot bolts. In replacing, check that the spring washer is included in its proper position (under the nut next to the twistgrip body).

Removal of the throttle twistgrip follows the method already described for replacing a throttle cable. (*See also* Fig. 23.)

Note. Refer also to Figs. 37 and 38 for cable details.

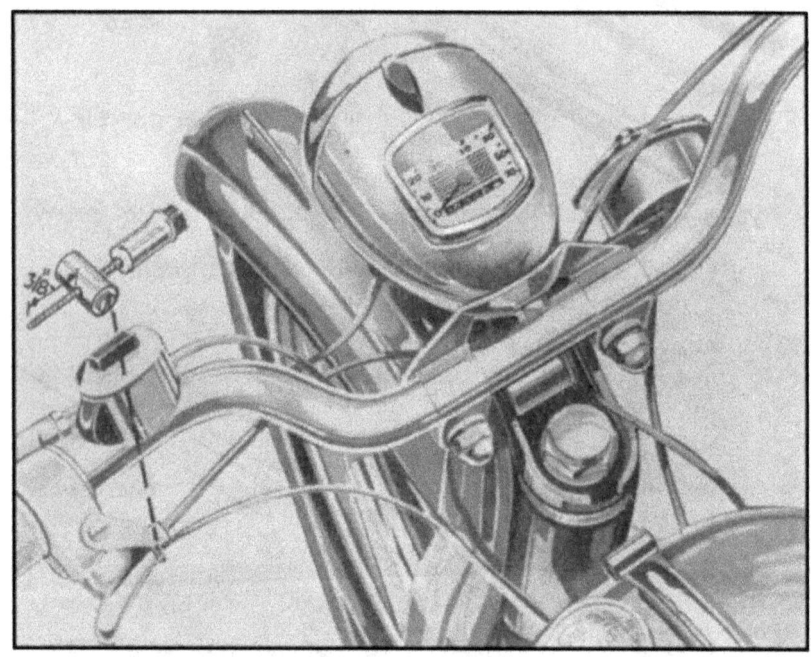

FIG. 27. THE DECOMPRESSOR CABLE
This terminates in a solderless nipple at handlebar end. Cable should protrude ⅜ in. through end fitting.

Special Note re Throttle Cable on Later Models. The following special notes apply to machines with the new type covered twistgrip (from model 268 490/286 207). When fitting the new cable with 5 mm nipple into the grip, care must be taken to ensure that the distance between the ends of the sleeve and the ends of the cable, when the carburettor slide is in the slow-running position, is 40 mm (1·4 in.). The recommended method of fitting is—

1. Remove twistgrip housing from handlebar.
2. Insert casing into square aperture of the twistgrip. Place cable through slit and locate the nipple in the nipple seating.

DETAILED MAINTENANCE 47

3. Fit the twistgrip to the housing away from the handlebar, pass cable through slit in housing and adjust sleeve. File the housing, as necessary, to ensure an internal diameter of 26·5 to 27 mm (1·052–1·073 in.).
4. Hold the cable firmly. Replace twistgrip on handlebar and secure housing with clamp screw.
5. Turn the twistgrip $\frac{1}{4}$ turn open (accelerating) so that the bridge lies opposite the braking spring.
6. Now adjust the screw for the brake spring and tighten nut to lock.

Fitting Gear-change Cable on Quickly-S/2 (and all other three-speed models). This cable is best removed by taking off the right cover of the magneto, engaging third gear, and tightening completely the cable adjusters. Then separate cap from the dog (with a screwdriver) and pull out cables. It may be helpful to remove the carburettor. Connect both nipples of the Bowden cable with thin binding wire (about 5 ft long) and pull out cables upwards one after the other. Loosen adjusting screw on the twistgrip, remove twistgrip from handlebars and withdraw nipple ends of cables.

To replace, pull through cables separately with thin wire. The marked cable (red spot or hole in cable adjuster) must always face to the twistgrip rear; cables must not be crossed; and the longer sides of the nipples must point downwards. To mount the lower cable, third gear must be engaged.

2. FRONT AND REAR BRAKES

For the renewal of brake linings the wheel must be removed from the frame (*see* Section 3) and the brake backplate detached from the wheel. The brake backplate on the front wheel can be removed by holding the brake lever and unscrewing the hexagon nut on the backplate with a spanner. Striking the right-hand bearing cone with a rubber hammer or block of wood should loosen the backplate, which can then be removed. The action is essentially similar in the case of the back wheel except that the first step is to remove the large circlip in the hub.

The front wheel assembly differs on models up to 482 754/522 989 and subsequent models. (*See* Figs. 28 and 29.) The two types can be identified from the fact that the spindle in the former case is in the form of a long bolt while in later models there is a rod threaded for a nut at each end. Main differences from the point of brake lining renewal are the springs and different part numbers for the shoes and linings. Similar differences are observed in the case of the rear wheel brakes. (*See* Figs. 30 and 31.)

The shoes can be removed by unclipping the springs or spring with pliers. The old linings can then be removed by cutting off the heads of the rivets inside the linings and being punched out clear. The new linings are assembled by fitting and clenching them over the centre rivets first, then working outwards to each end making sure that the whole length of lining is bedded down flat on the shoe.

48 THE BOOK OF THE NSU QUICKLY

Assembly of the two-spring unit is best done by attaching one spring to both shoes at the pivot end, then fitting the shoes in place, and finally engaging the second spring (which may already be hooked into one shoe for convenience). With the single-spring unit it will usually be found

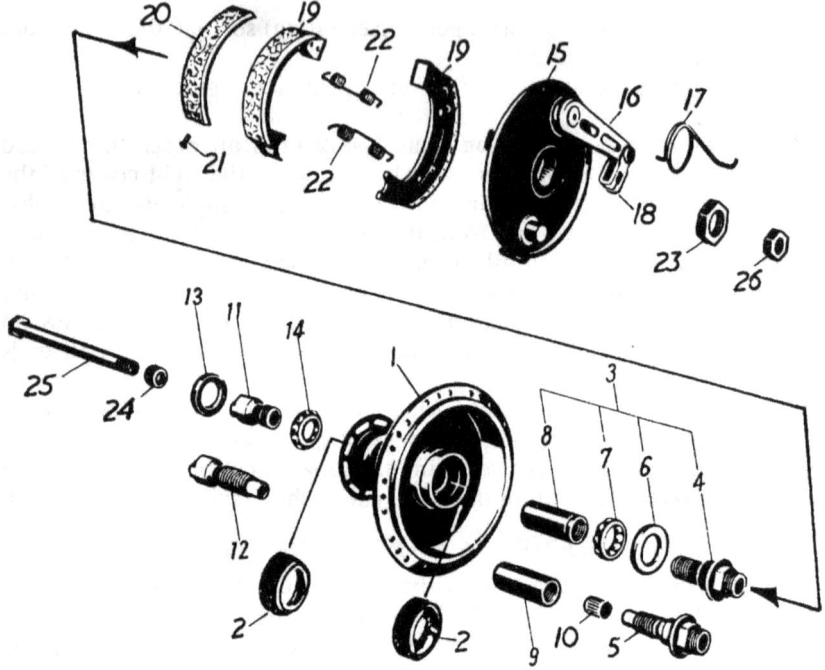

FIG. 28. FRONT HUB ASSEMBLY (UP TO MODEL 482 754/522 989)

1. Hub
2. Ball race cups
3. Cone assembly
4. Cone (early models)
5. Cone (late models)
6. Seal ring
7. Ball cage and balls
8. Spacer (early models)
9. Spacer (late models)
10. Tolerance ring
11. Cone (early models)
12. Cone (late models)
13. Seal ring
14. Ball cage and balls
15. Brake plate
16. Brake lever
17. Spring
18. Yoke
19. Brake shoe
20. Brake lining
21. Rivets (16)
22. Spring
23. Nut
24. Ring
25. Spindle
26. Nut

easiest to hook the spring in one shoe, fit both shoes in place and then engage the spring in the second shoe with pointed-nose pliers.

3. WHEELS

Standard 26 × 2 in. wheels are used on the N and S models and 23 × 2¼ in. wheels on the N/23 and S/23. In both cases the rear wheel

[*Contd. on p.* 55]

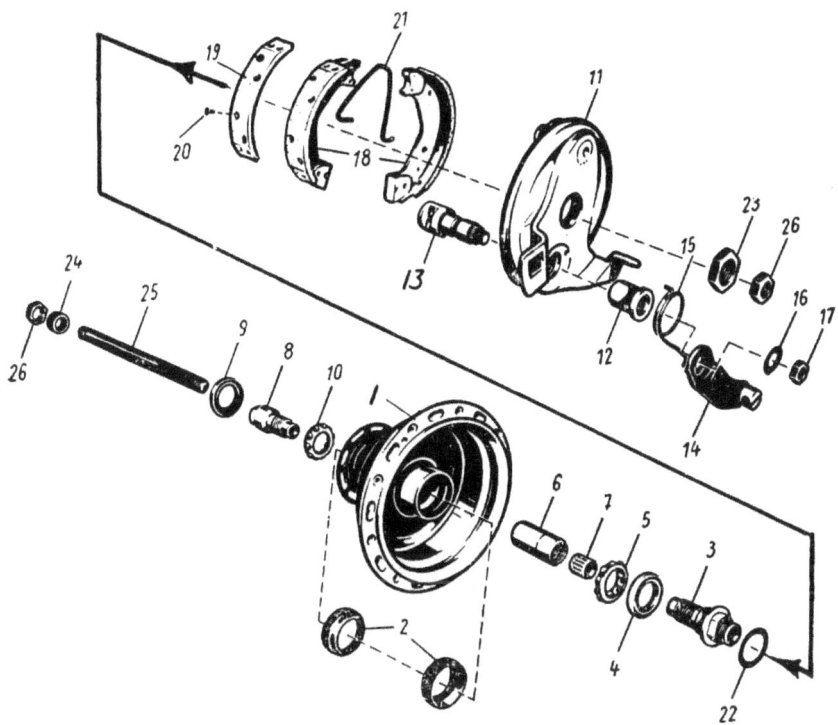

FIG. 29. FRONT HUB ASSEMBLY (MODELS SUBSEQUENT TO 482 755/522 990)

1. Hub
2. Ball race cups
3. Cone
4. Seal ring
5. Ball cage and balls
6. Spacer
7. Tolerance ring
8. Cone
9. Seal ring
10. Ball cage and balls
11. Brake plate
12. Bush
13. Brake operating cam
14. Brake lever
15. Spring
16. Spring washer
17. Nut
18. Brake shoe
19. Brake lining
20. Rivets (16)
21. Spring
22. Shim
23. Nut
24. Ring
25. Spindle
26. Nut

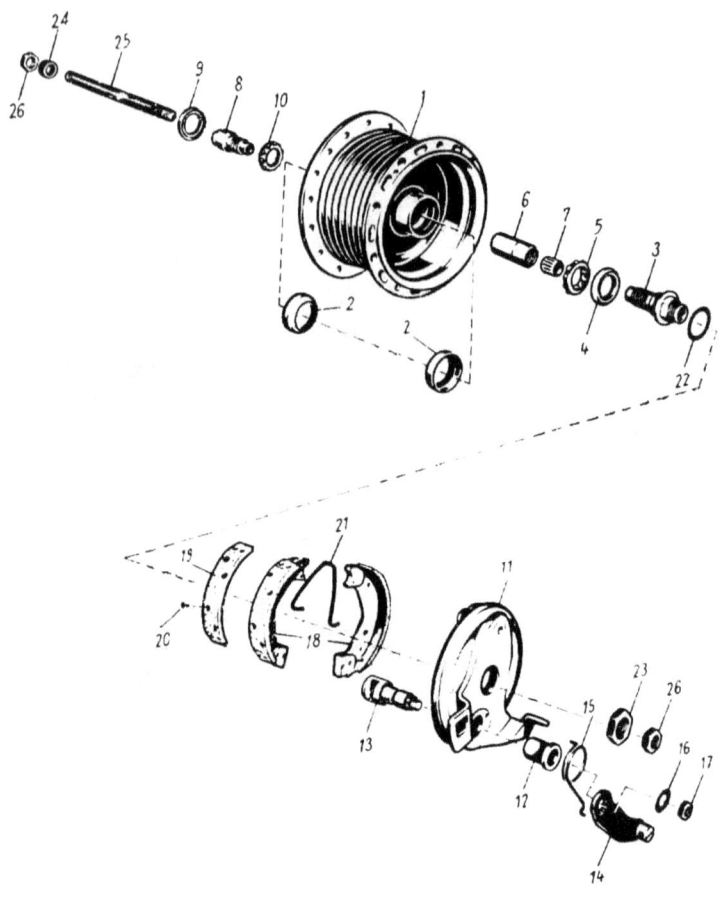

FIG. 29A. FRONT HUB QUICKLY 23 MODELS N AND S

1. Hub
2. Ball race
3. Cone
4. Seal ring
5. Ball cage
6. Spacer
7. Tolerance ring
8. Cone
9. Seal ring
10. Ball cage
11. Brake plate
12. Bush
13. Brake operating cam
14. Brake lever
15. Spring
16. Spring washer
17. Nut
18. Brake shoe
19. Lining
20. Rivet
21. Spring
22. Shim
23. Nut
24. Spacer bush
25. Spindle
26. Nut

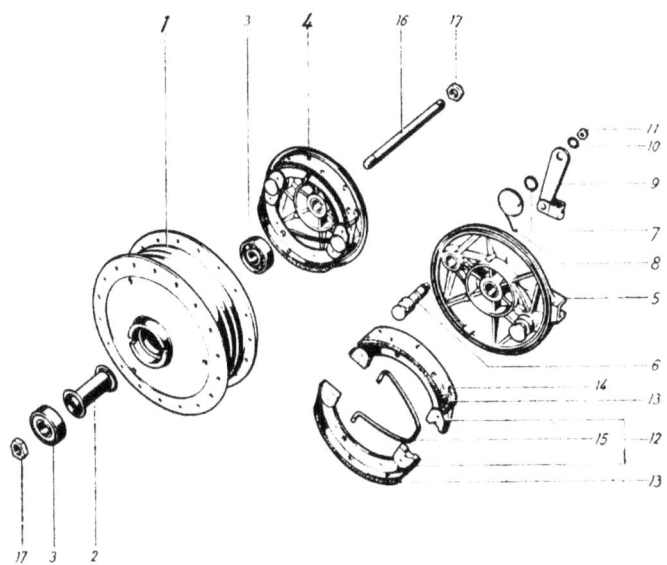

FIG. 29B. FRONT HUB QUICKLY 23 S/2 AND QUICKLY F

1. Hub
2. Spacer
3. Bearing
4. Brake
5. Brake plate
6. Brake operating cam
7. Seal ring
8. Spring
9. Brake lever
10. Spring washer
11. Nut
12. Brake shoe
13. Brake lining
14. Rivet
15. Spring
16. Spindle
17. Nut

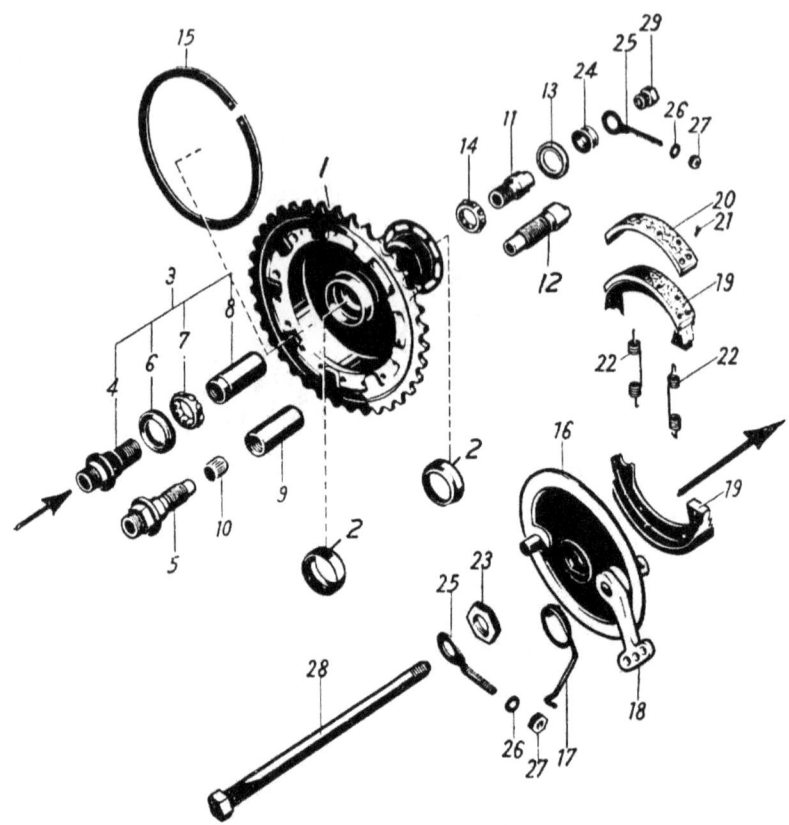

FIG. 30. REAR HUB ASSEMBLY (MODELS UP TO 482 754/522 989)

1. Hub
2. Ball race cups
3. Cone assembly
4. Cone (early models)
5. Cone (later models)
6. Seal ring
7. Ball cage and balls
8. Spacer (early models)
9. Spacer (late models)
10. Tolerance ring
11. Cone (early models)
12. Cone (late models)
13. Seal ring
14. Ball cage and balls
15. Circlip
16. Brake plate
17. Spring
18. Brake lever
19. Brake shoe
20. Brake lining
21. Rivets (16)
22. Spring
23. Nut
24. Spacer
25. Chain adjuster
26. Spring washer
27. Nut
28. Spindle
29. Nut

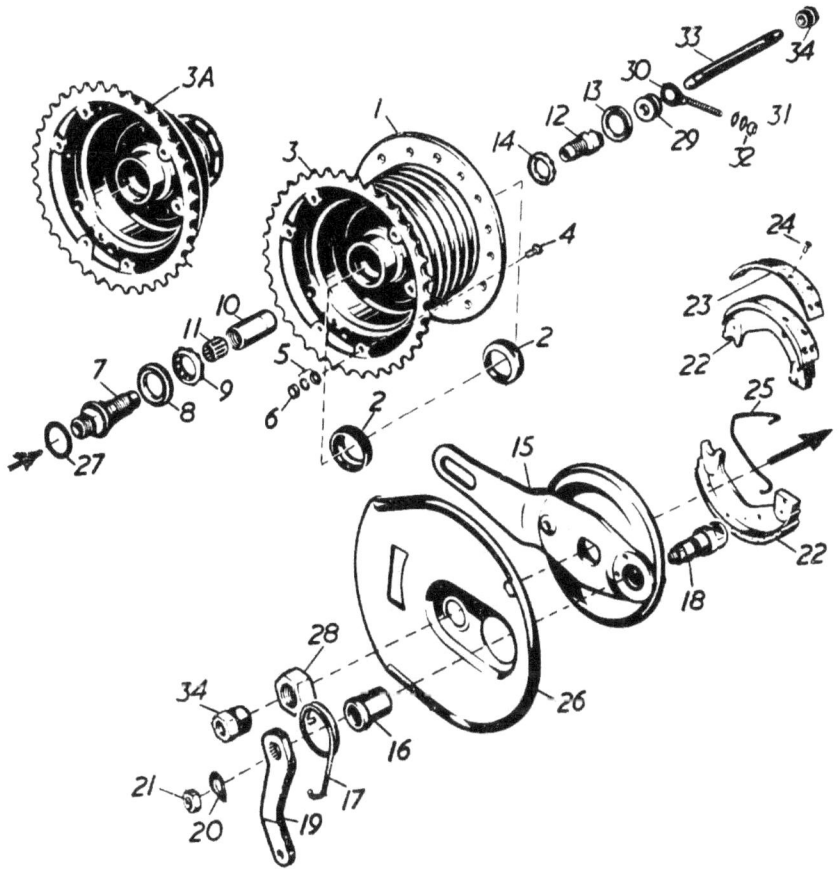

FIG. 31. REAR HUB ASSEMBLY (MODELS SUBSEQUENT TO 482 755/522 990)

1. Hub
2. Ball race cups
3. Sprocket (L model)
3a. Sprocket (N and S models)
4. Bolt
5. Spring washers
6. Nut
7. Cone
8. Seal ring
9. Ball cage and balls
10. Spacer
11. Tolerance ring
12. Cone
13. Seal ring
14. Ball cage and balls
15. Rear plate
    Bush
17. Spring
18. Brake operating cam
19. Brake lever
20. Spring washer
21. Nut
22. Brake shoe
23. Brake lining
24. Rivets (16)
25. Spring
26. Cover
27. Shim
28. Nut
29. Spacer
30. Chain adjuster
31. Spring washer
32. Nut
33. Spindle
34. Nut

53

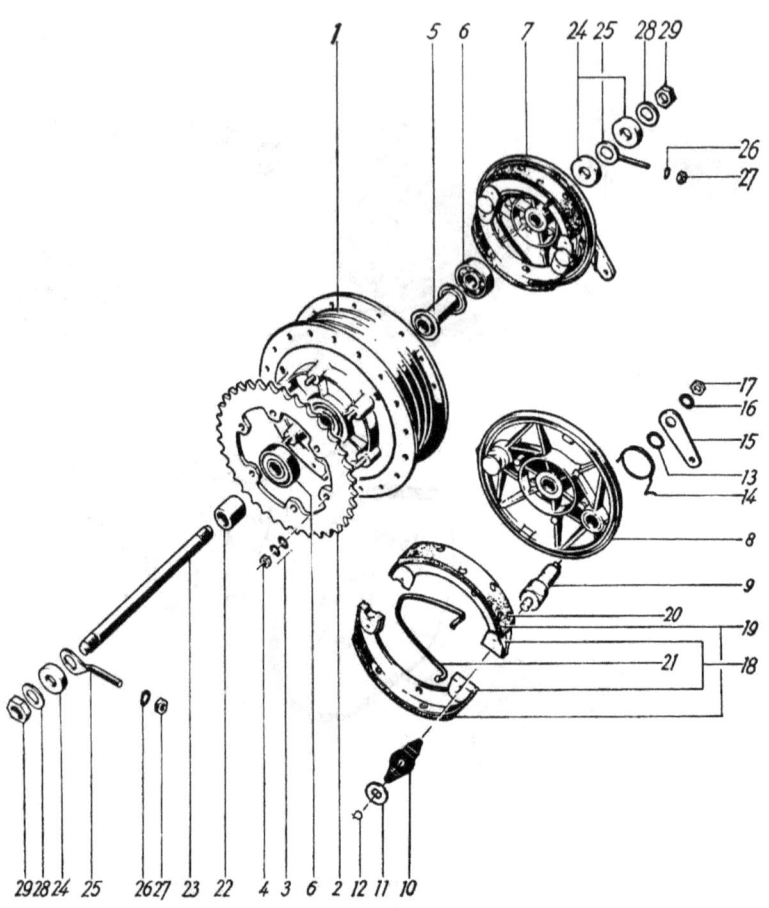

FIG. 31A. REAR HUB ASSEMBLY S/2 AND F MODELS

1. Hub
2. Sprocket
3. Spring washer
4. Nut
5. Spacer
6. Ball bearing
7. Rear brake
8. Brake plate
9. Brake operating cam
10. Spring
11. Washer
12. Locking washer
13. Seal ring
14. Spring
15. Brake lever
16. Spring washer
17. Nut
18. Brake shoe
19. Brake lining
20. Rivet
21. Spring
22. Spacing washer (left)
23. Spindle
24. Spacing washer
25. Chain adjusting screw
26. Spring washer
27. Nut
28. Spring washer
29. Nut

DETAILED MAINTENANCE 55

differs from the front wheel in the hub design and also in the thickness and length of spokes. The front and rear wheels of the 26-in. L model are distinguished from those of the N and S models by the thicker hub section continued right across the wheel; also the spokes are the same length on either side of the wheel ($9\frac{3}{4}$ in. or 235 mm) instead of unequal lengths (left-hand $10\frac{3}{8}$ in. or 263 mm; right-hand $9\frac{1}{4}$ in. or 235 mm). Both the S 23 and S/2 23 have full width hubs but in the case of the two-seat model the brake area on each wheel is increased to 6·5 sq in. (as compared with 3·4 sq in.) and the rear tyre size is 23 × $2\frac{1}{2}$ in. On the N 23 and S 23 the rims are of steel (enamelled and plated, respectively); and on the S/2 23 the rims are of aluminium alloy.

The front wheel on all models is mounted on swinging links bearing against compression springs housed in the forks (*see* Section 4). To remove the wheel it is first necessary to disconnect the front brake cable completely from the right-hand side and slacken off the pinch bolts on each side. (*See* Fig. 35.) The spindle nut is then removed from the right-hand side (or the right-hand nut removed in the case of models subsequent to 482 754/522 989) and the spindle knocked right through, and removed from the left-hand side. The wheel then drops out free.

If a speedometer is fitted this is mounted against the left-hand side of the hub and also drops free with the withdrawal of the spindle. Where there is no speedometer two spacer rings are fitted in lieu of it and these must be replaced on the left-hand bearing cone in refitting the wheel. The brake backplate must also be brought to bear against the anchorage on the swinging arm on the right-hand side of the hub.

The rear wheel is removed in a similar manner, starting by disconnecting the brake rod from the brake arm (*see* Fig. 32) in the case of the N and S models, or by disconnecting the Bowden cable in the case of the L model. First remove the locking loop in each case and slacken off the chain adjuster nuts each side. The axle nut can then be removed from the right-hand side and the spindle driven out to the left, allowing the wheel to drop free. If now slid forwards the chain can be removed from the rear sprocket and the complete wheel removed. (*See* Fig. 33.)

Replacement follows in the reverse order, readjusting the chain tension correctly and making sure that these align the wheel true in the forks. The brake plate must bear against the step on the rear frame (N and S models); or against the step on the rear swinging arm (L model).

When attention is required to the hub bearings or seal, remove the wheel and brake backplate. (*See* Section 2.) Hold the left-hand bearing cone with a suitable spanner and unscrew it. If the hub is then rested over the open jaws of a vice the right-hand cone can be knocked out with a suitable drift or flat punch laid against the inner edge of the cone. If the two ball bearing rings are to be withdrawn an extractor must be used for this purpose. Details of the assembly should be clear from Figs. 28 and 29 which show the front wheel hub; and Figs. 30 and 31 on the rear wheel hub.

Removal and Replacement of Front Wheel: Quickly F. The correct procedure with the Quickly F (*see* Fig. 29B) is to disconnect the brake cable and remove the adjustment screw, also remove the speedometer drive spindle. The axle nut should then be removed, both lock nuts loosened and the knock-out spindle pushed out. Lift the brake unit out of its bearing, when the wheel can be removed.

Refitting the wheel follows in the reverse order, the only point to watch being that the speedometer cable must be correctly fed into place.

If the brake shoes are to be replaced the wheel is removed, as above,

FIG. 32. REAR BRAKE IS OPERATED BY BACK-PEDALLING ACTION
  A. Brake lever (actuated by pedals)
  B. Brake rod (Bowden cable on L model)
  C. Adjuster

and both brake shoes pushed towards the cam with a screwdriver. The brake anchor plate can then be removed and the shoes withdrawn.

When replacing, the shoes must be offered up into position in the position of a wide "vee" to engage the return spring in each shoe, then pushed downwards to lie flat. Check that the return spring locates in the groove on the brake anchor pin before completing the assembly.

Removal and Stripping of Rear Wheel: Quickly F. (*See* Fig. 31A.) The first step is to disconnect the brake linkage by removing the split pin and to loosen the chain tensioner. Then remove one axle nut and drive or push out the knock-out axle. The wheel can then be removed by pushing forward so that the chain can be removed.

DETAILED MAINTENANCE

Refitting the wheel follows in the reverse order, taking care that the long distance-piece is on the sprocket side of the wheel. Chain tension should be adjusted with one person sitting on the saddle, the tension required corresponding to a slack of $\frac{5}{8}$ to $\frac{3}{4}$ inch. In this respect chain adjustment differs from that on other Quickly models where the same slack is required *without* anyone sitting on the machine.

If disassembly of the rear wheel is to be taken further, after removing the wheel, remove the brake shoes as previously described for the front wheel. To replace brake linings, drill out all the rivets so that the old

FIG. 33. REAR WHEEL DETAIL
A. Chain tension adjusters (slacken off to remove wheel)
B. Knock-out spindle
C. Spring link (detach to remove chain)
D. Rear brake arm

shoes can be removed. Rivetting on of new shoes should start at the middle of the lining, working towards each end in turn so that the linings are forced tightly onto the shoes along their whole length.

To remove the wheel bearings an internal extractor is needed. When replacing or refitting a new bearing, grease the bearing first and use a metal tube to drive the bearing into place. Be sure that the bearing is positioned the right way round (the sealed side of the bearing facing outwards).

When replacing brake shoes, assemble as for the front wheel and again note that the return spring positions properly in the groove in the brake anchor pin.

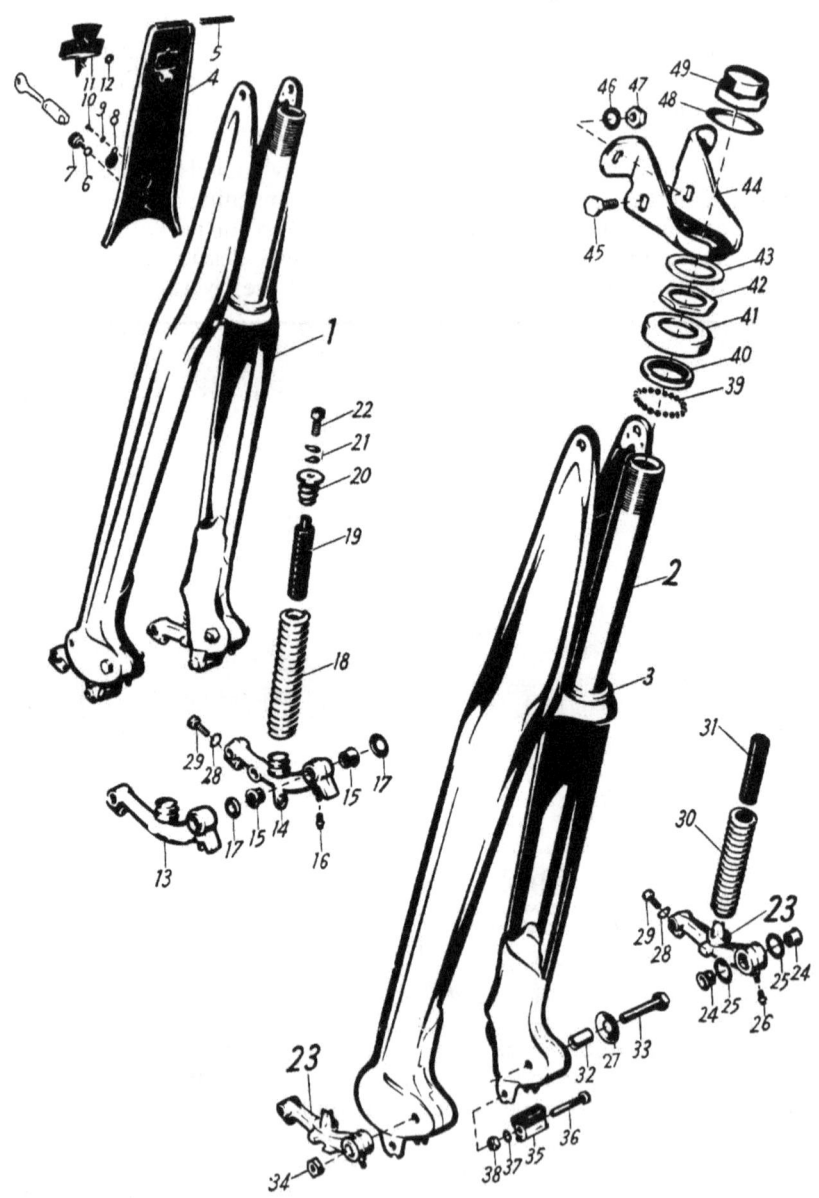

Fig. 34. Spring Forks N and S Models

4. SUSPENSION, FRAME AND FORKS

The front spring-fork assembly has been modified in detail on progressive models (*see* Appendix II) although the operating principle remains

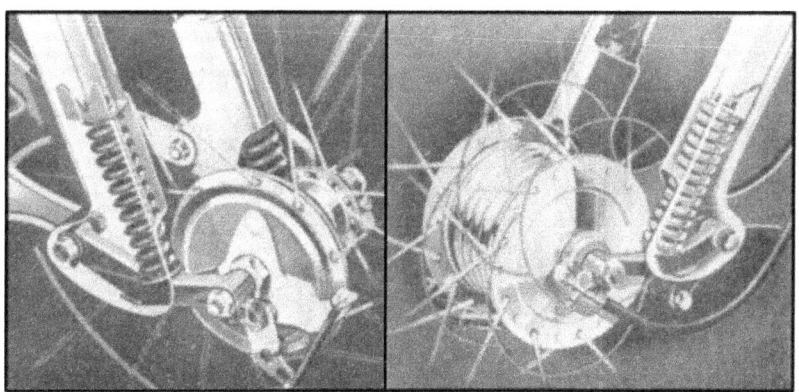

FIG. 35. N AND S MODELS HUB (*left*) AND L MODEL HUB (*right*)
Essential difference lies in the appearance, the brake area being the same.

identical. The appearance of the hubs of the N and S models and the L model is shown in Fig. 35. Details of the component assembly of the spring hub in late models N and S (subsequent to 482 755/522 989) are shown in Fig. 34; and details of the L model spring-fork unit in Fig. 36.

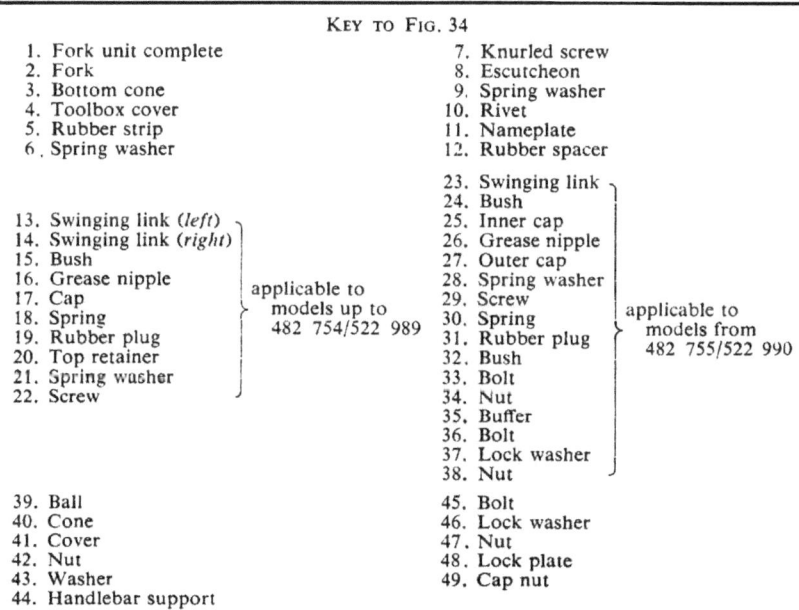

KEY TO FIG. 34

1. Fork unit complete
2. Fork
3. Bottom cone
4. Toolbox cover
5. Rubber strip
6. Spring washer

7. Knurled screw
8. Escutcheon
9. Spring washer
10. Rivet
11. Nameplate
12. Rubber spacer

13. Swinging link (*left*)
14. Swinging link (*right*)
15. Bush
16. Grease nipple
17. Cap
18. Spring
19. Rubber plug
20. Top retainer
21. Spring washer
22. Screw

applicable to models up to 482 754/522 989

23. Swinging link
24. Bush
25. Inner cap
26. Grease nipple
27. Outer cap
28. Spring washer
29. Screw
30. Spring
31. Rubber plug
32. Bush
33. Bolt
34. Nut
35. Buffer
36. Bolt
37. Lock washer
38. Nut

applicable to models from 482 755/522 990

39. Ball
40. Cone
41. Cover
42. Nut
43. Washer
44. Handlebar support

45. Bolt
46. Lock washer
47. Nut
48. Lock plate
49. Cap nut

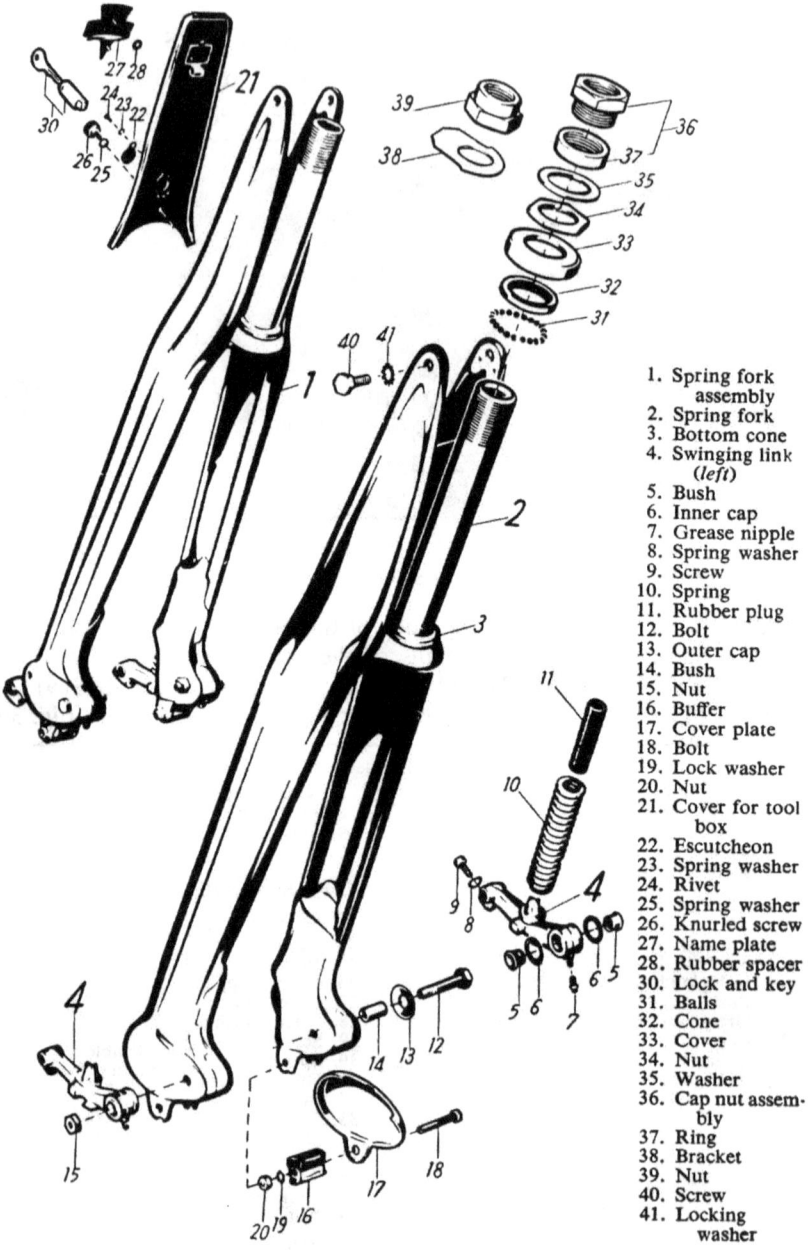

1. Spring fork assembly
2. Spring fork
3. Bottom cone
4. Swinging link (*left*)
5. Bush
6. Inner cap
7. Grease nipple
8. Spring washer
9. Screw
10. Spring
11. Rubber plug
12. Bolt
13. Outer cap
14. Bush
15. Nut
16. Buffer
17. Cover plate
18. Bolt
19. Lock washer
20. Nut
21. Cover for tool box
22. Escutcheon
23. Spring washer
24. Rivet
25. Spring washer
26. Knurled screw
27. Name plate
28. Rubber spacer
30. Lock and key
31. Balls
32. Cone
33. Cover
34. Nut
35. Washer
36. Cap nut assembly
37. Ring
38. Bracket
39. Nut
40. Screw
41. Locking washer

FIG. 36. SPRING FORK ASSEMBLY L MODEL

DETAILED MAINTENANCE

In all cases removal of the pivoted links is similar, first removing the front wheel and then unscrewing the nuts on the pivot bolts and knocking out the bolts. The right-hand pivoted link carries the brake cable carrier, which is removed by unscrewing. The springs are then released by unscrewing the small hexagon-headed bolt at the top end of each spring,

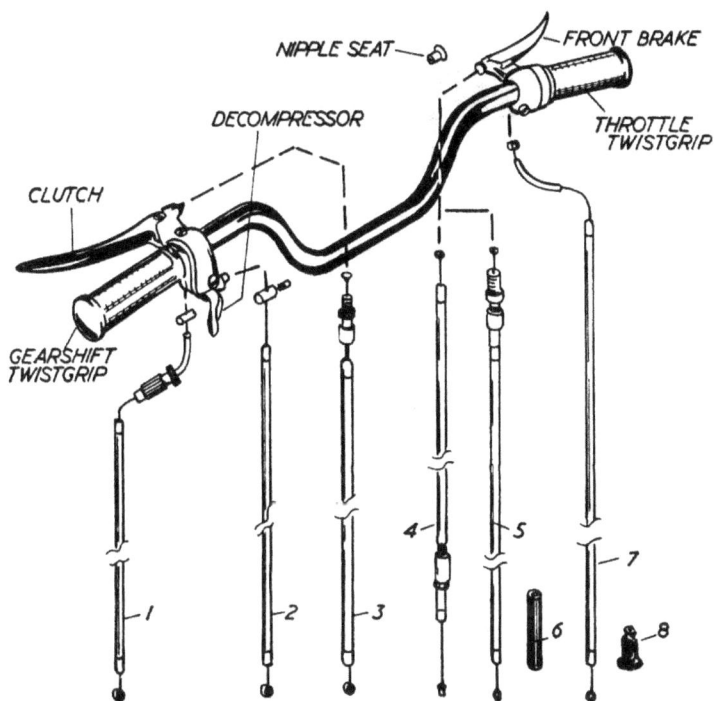

FIG. 37. HANDLEBARS AND CABLES N AND S MODELS

1. Gearchange cable
2. Decompressor cable
3. Clutch cable
4. Front brake cable (early models with adjuster at wheel end)
5. Front brake cable (late models)
6. Rubber sleeve fitting front brake cable end
7. Throttle cable
8. Rubber cover for throttle cable (carburettor end)

where applicable (up to model 482 754/522 989). On subsequent models, and all L models, the pivoted links with springs may be removed once the pivot bolts are knocked out.

The bushes in the pivoted links are press fitted and can be knocked out with a suitable drift or punch, if requiring replacement. New bushes are pressed in place and then reamed to size. The required bush diameter should be checked carefully as this varies with the model series. Earlier machines require a finished bush size of 11·02 mm (0·434 in.) and later machines a reamed size of 12·02 mm (0·473 in.) to match.

Handlebar assembly for the N and S models is shown in Fig. 37; and the L model in Fig. 38. Again there are differences in detail design on the earlier models, particularly as regards the twistgrips. Removal of the twistgrips is discussed in Section 1. Stripping of the handlebars follows logically; also removal of the handlebars, when necessary.

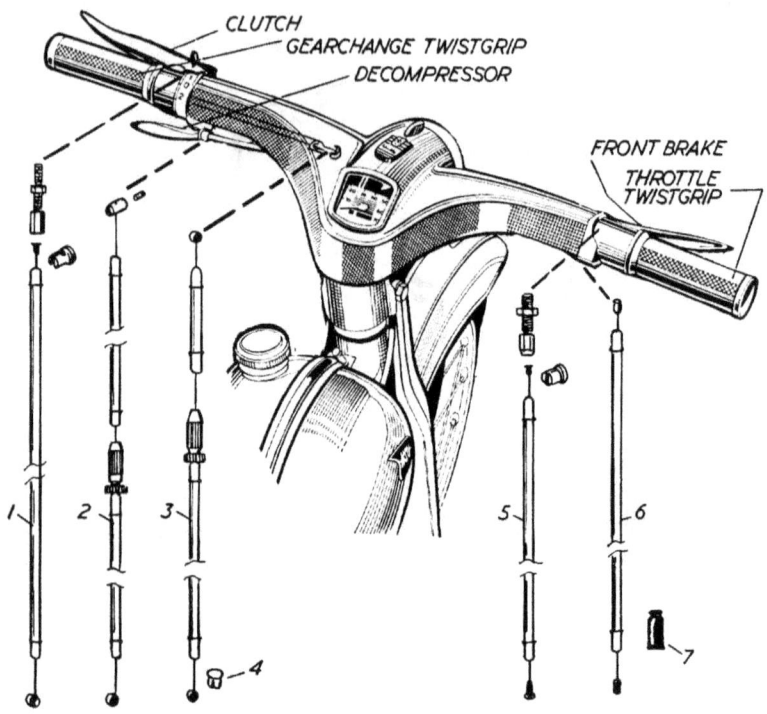

FIG. 38. HANDLEBARS AND CABLES L MODEL
1. Clutch cable
2. Decompressor cable
3. Gearchange cable
4. Sleeve (at end of gearchange cable)
5. Front brake cable
6. Throttle cable
7 Rubber cover for throttle cable (carburettor end)

The front forks may be removed by first removing the wheel. In the case of the N and S models the headlamp rim is then detached by removing the knurled screw, the leads disconnected and pulled out through the rubber grommet. The hexagon nut on the fork stem is then removed, together with its lock washer, and the two hexagon-headed bolts, cap nuts and lock washers on the mounting clips. The handlebars are then removed and laid aside, and the headlamp detached. The fork is then released by undoing the lock nut on the stem, allowing the forks to drop out downwards.

DETAILED MAINTENANCE 63

The steering head cones are now exposed. The upper cone cover, upper cone and balls can be withdrawn, also the balls from the lower race. The two races can then be removed, if necessary by driving out with a suitable drift or punch. The lower cone is fitted to the fork stem and can be driven off with a flat punch or prised off with a screwdriver, if necessary to replace. (*See also* Figs. 34 and 36.)

Reassembly consists of driving the lower cone in place on the stem, e.g. using a metal tube which fits snugly over the stem, refitting the two races

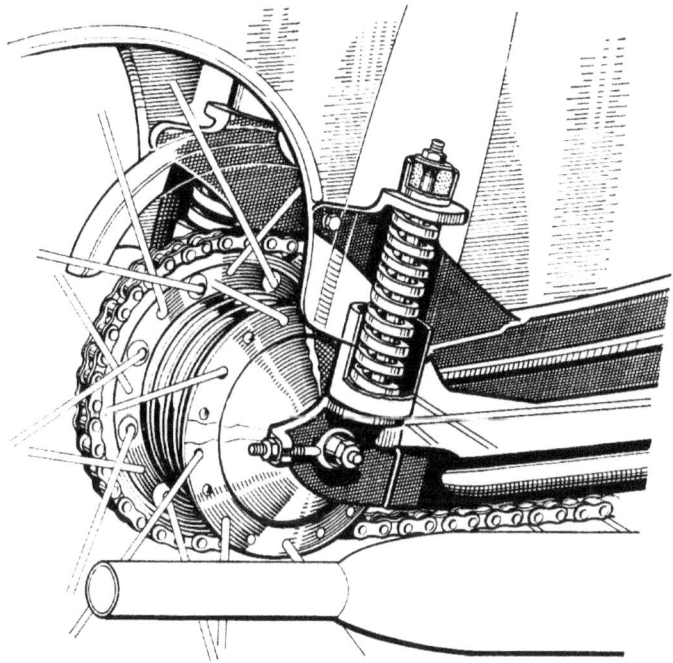

FIG. 39. REAR SUSPENSION OF L MODEL

in the top and bottom of the steering head and then adding the balls. Twenty-one 5 mm diameter balls are used in each race, bedded in grease. The upper cone and cover is then added and the forks offered up and slid in carefully upwards, and secured with the locknut. Head bearings are then adjusted so as not to allow play in the forks, but with sufficient freedom of movement that the weight of the forks, with wheel fitted temporarily, will swing them to full lock on either side.

Whilst the basic frame is essentially similar on all models, detail changes occur after model 482 755/522 990. Also the L model frame incorporates additional fittings for the rear assembly. The frame itself is of pressed-steel construction in the form of a box girder giving exceptional rigidity for a low weight and is unlikely to receive damage except in the case of a serious accident. A replacement item is the only satisfactory solution in the case of a damaged frame. A particularly important maintenance feature is that unless the three engine-mounting bolts are kept tight—checked at regular intervals (preferably weekly) and retightened as necessary—vibration may cause the bolt holes to elongate and eventually the metal to fracture. Later models have locking plates replacing the star washers under the nuts to lessen the possibility of loosening.

Rear-wheel mounting for the N and S is of the bicycle type, the spindle being bolted directly to the frame unit. On the L model the rear wheel is mounted on a swinging-arm unit pivoted to the frame and sprung with compression springs mounted on the ends of the arms and bearing lug fittings on the frame. (*See* Fig. 39.) The bottom of each spring rests in a cap and at the top is a rubber shock absorber, the complete assembly being mounted on a connecting pin or bolt threaded at the top end to take a threaded washer and nut. The spring can be removed by undoing this nut and washer and withdrawing the spindle downwards, taking care not to lose the spacing washer, spring washer and C-washer under the cap (assembled in that order with the spacing washer next to the swinging-arm lug).

Rear Suspension: Quickly F. If it is necessary to dismantle the rear suspension, remove the circlips from the lower end of each suspension strut, remove the rear wheel as described on p. 56 and knock out the pivot pins of both rear shock absorbers. Unscrew the top cover of each strut in turn, together with the locknuts, when the suspension units may be extracted in a downwards direction.

To take the suspension units apart, hold the centre rod by tightening the lock nut, slide off the protective tube and extract the spring. Reassemble in the reverse order, but always replace the springs in pairs. On reassembly of the complete suspension unit, make sure that the centring discs on the centre rod are fitted in the correct sequence.

To remove the swinging levers, strip down as above (without disassembling the suspension units themselves) and pull out the brake adjustment screw. Undo the lower attachment of the suspension strut, remove circlip from the pivot pin and knock out the pin.

Reassemble in the reverse order, paying particular attention to the fact that the two spacing washers of equal thickness are fitted on either side of the fulcrum boss and that the lever swings freely without play.

5. CHAIN

The final drive or transmission of power between the gearbox and rear wheel is by roller chain of generous dimensions. A 112 link chain is standard. The chain should give no trouble provided—

1. It is never allowed to run dry (weekly oiling of the rollers is recommended).

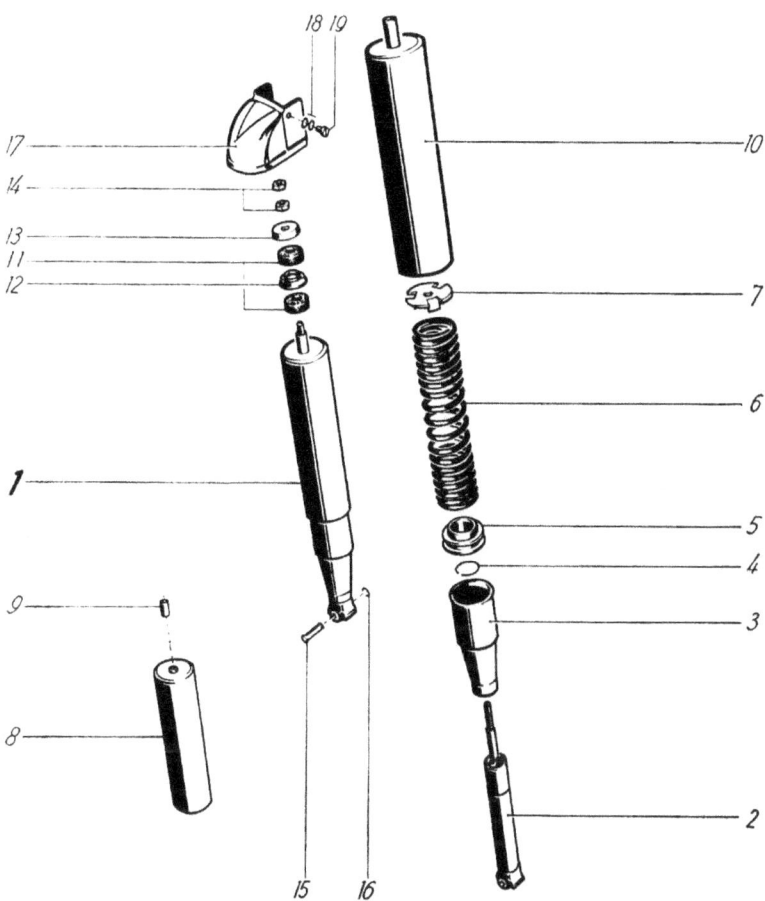

FIG. 39A. QUICKLY F REAR WHEEL SUSPENSION

1. Suspension unit
2. Shock absorber
3. Bush
4. Spring slip
5. Supporting ring
6. Rear spring
7. Centring washer
8. Tube
9. Distance bush
10. Tube
11. Rubber ring
12. and 13. Centring cups
14. Nut
15. Pin
16. Lock washer
17. Cover plate
18. Spring washer
19. Cheesehead screw

2. It is cleaned regularly by washing in paraffin and re-greased before replacing.
3. The chain tension is checked periodically and readjusted, as necessary.

The total free movement of "lift" on the bottom length of the chain, with the machine on its wheels and unloaded, should be between $\frac{5}{8}$ and $\frac{3}{4}$ in. (*See* Fig. 20.) If adjustment is required both rear wheel spindle nuts should be slackened-off and the chain-adjuster nuts tightened an equal amount each side. (*See* Fig. 19.) It is important that both adjusters are tightened the same amount as otherwise the alignment of the wheel will be affected. When the chain sag is again correct, retighten the wheel spindle nuts. Since adjustment of chain tension moves the rear wheel relative to the frame this may affect the rear brake operation, which should be checked and readjusted if necessary.

To remove the chain—e.g. for cleaning or as a preliminary to removing the rear wheel—rotate the pedals to bring the spring link on to the rear sprocket and prise off the spring with a screwdriver. When replacing the chain, again assemble with the connecting link on the rear sprocket inserted from the back so that the spring clip is on the *outside*. The closed end of the spring should always face the direction of travel of the chain (Fig. 20).

6. CARBURETTOR AND AIR FILTER

An exploded view of the carburettor and air filter is shown in detail in Fig. 40. The carburettor is attached directly to the cylinder with two nuts and a gasket sandwiched between the two mating flanges. The air filter is mounted in the frame section, attached by a thin bolt from the choke cover on the left-hand side passing through to terminate in a nut and spring washer on the right-hand side. Removing this nut and washer and withdrawing the bolt enables the air filter to be dropped out for cleaning. Connexion between the air filter and the carburettor intake is by a rubber elbow which is merely pushed on at each end.

Normally no adjustment whatever should be required on the carburettor, the manufacturer's original settings being consistent with optimum performance and minimum fuel consumption. The mixture is controlled by the setting of the jet needle located in the appropriate groove by a spring circlip. If removed for any reason care should be taken that it is reassembled in the same groove as originally found. Also care must be taken not to bend the needle as this will upset the mixture setting. Wear may be apparent on the needle after long service which could affect the mixture, but moving it down to the next groove should compensate for this.

An over-rich mixture, indicated by a black and velvety sooty deposit on the spark plug, can be caused by the needle being set too high, the main jet being enlarged (e.g. through being reamed out oversize accidentally by cleaning with a wire instead of a bristle); a sticking float (or float punctured and "sunk," or wrongly placed on its needle); or a clogged

DETAILED MAINTENANCE

air filter. A positive check for over-rich mixture is to close the fuel tap with the engine running and leave the throttle setting undisturbed at a little above normal tick-over. If the engine speeds up markedly just before it dies out through lack of fuel, the mixture setting is on the rich side (too much fuel, or not enough air).

An over-lean mixture, on the other hand, will tend to produce cutting

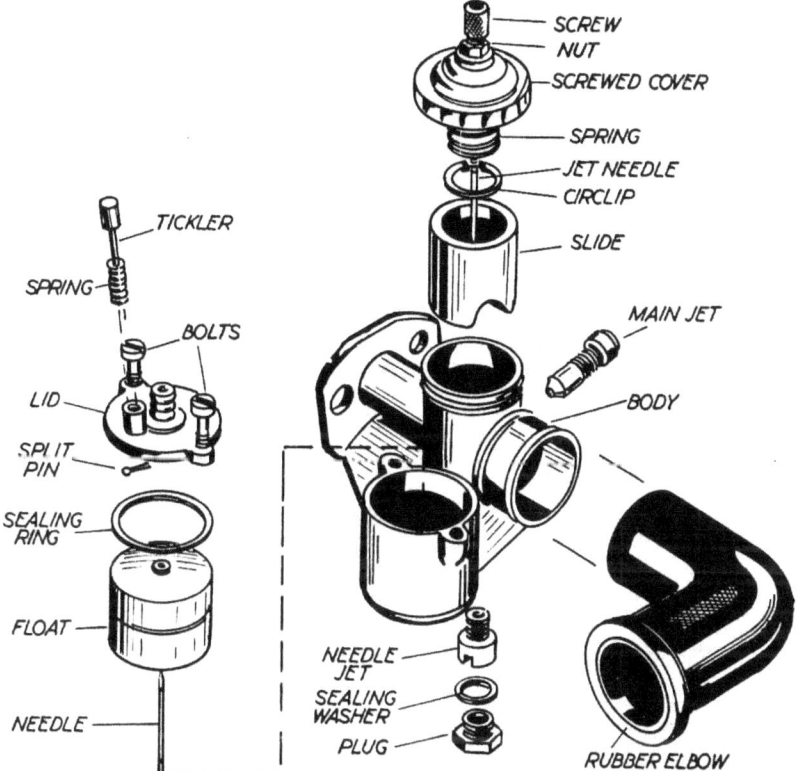

FIG. 40. AN EXPLODED VIEW OF THE CARBURETTOR USED ON THE TWO-SPEED MODELS SHOWING ALL PARTS

of the engine when running (particularly on opening up the throttle under load). The engine will also lack power and tend to overheat, which will also be evident by the appearance of the spark plug electrode (whitish in colour inside). The jet needle being placed too low will produce an over-lean mixture, but the most common cause is a blocked or partially blocked main jet. This may be produced by some solid matter which has been drawn into the jet or gummy oil deposits which have collected in the bottom of the carburettor. To guard against the latter possibility it is good practice to partially dismantle and wash out the carburettor with petrol from time to time, particularly if the machine has been left standing for a long period with fuel mixture in the carburettor. The main jet can be unscrewed for cleaning. Blowing through should be adequate to clear a partial blockage, but if the clogging is persistent, use a stiff, non-metallic bristle to remove it.

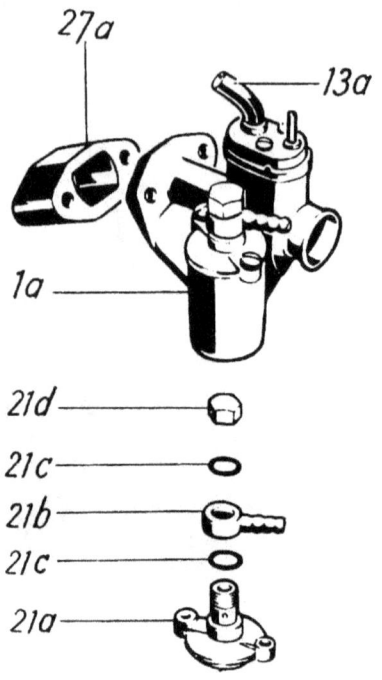

FIG. 40A. BING 1/12/127 CARBURETTOR FOR QUICKLY-S/2
1a. Body
13a. Tube
21a. Float chamber cover
21b. Swivelling hose adaptor
21c. Seal ring
21d. Nut
27a. Gasket

These represent different components relative to the standard carburettor. Other details as for Fig. 40 (with the exception of the hose). The same basic carburettor is retained on all later models but jet sizes may be modified and a longer induction gasket (27a) is used.

For starting purposes an over-rich mixture is required because the fuel does not vaporize so readily when the engine is cold. This effect is produced by operating the choke control to cut off most of the air supply temporarily so that the engine sucks in mainly fuel vapour. On later models the disc-type choke control on the bottom of the frame on the left-hand side is replaced by a choke fitting on the carburettor itself which is depressed to operate the choke and which automatically lifts again when the throttle is opened after starting. With the manual choke it is

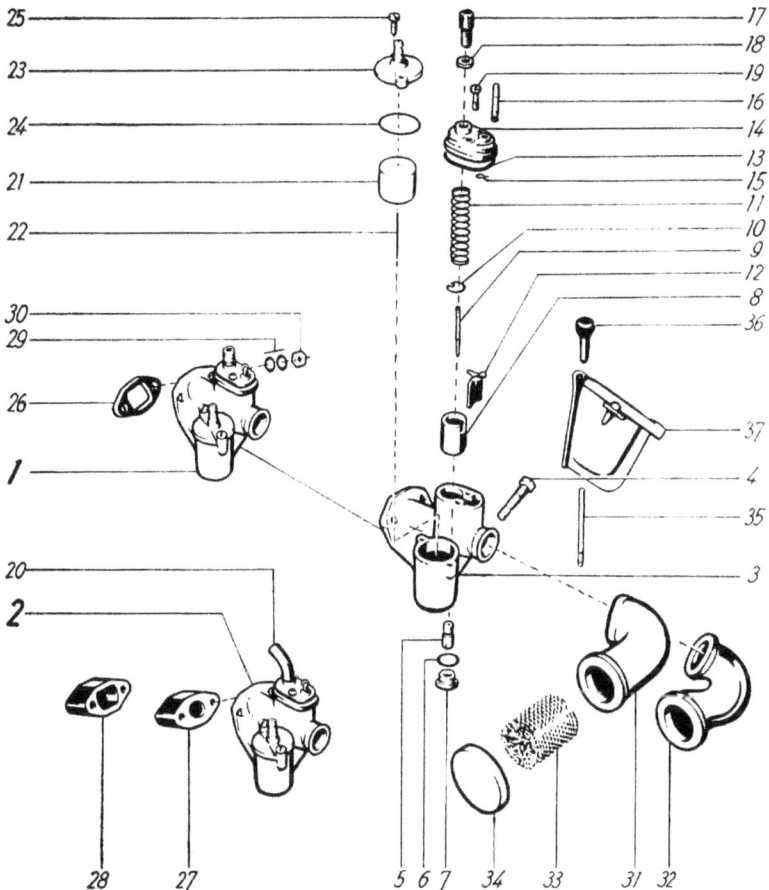

FIG. 40B. CARBURETTOR QUICKLY 23 MODELS N, S, S/2 AND F

3. Carburettor body
4. Main jet
5. Needle jet
6. Seal ring
7. Screw plug
8. Throttle slide
9. Jet needle
10. Circlip
11. Spring
12. Air slide
13. Gasket
14. Mixing chamber cap
15. Spring
16. Thrust rod
17. Adjusting screw
18. Nut
19. Bolt
20. Tube
21. Float
22. Float needle
23. Float chamber cover
24. Packing ring
25. Bolt
26, 27, 28. Gasket (different on different models)
29. Spring washer
30, 31. Nut
32. Hose
33. Wet-air filter
34. Cap
35. Pin
36. Knob
37. Leg-guard lid

important to remember to turn the choke to the "off" position as soon as the engine is running properly as otherwise an excessively rich mixture will continue to be drawn into the cylinder and the engine will not run properly.

The tickler on the carburettor is merely for the purpose of depressing the float and ensuring that the float chamber is completely full of fuel, ready for starting and running. If the tickler is held depressed, excess fuel will spill out of a small hole in the top of the float chamber as soon as it is full. Continued spillage of fuel through this hole with the tickler released

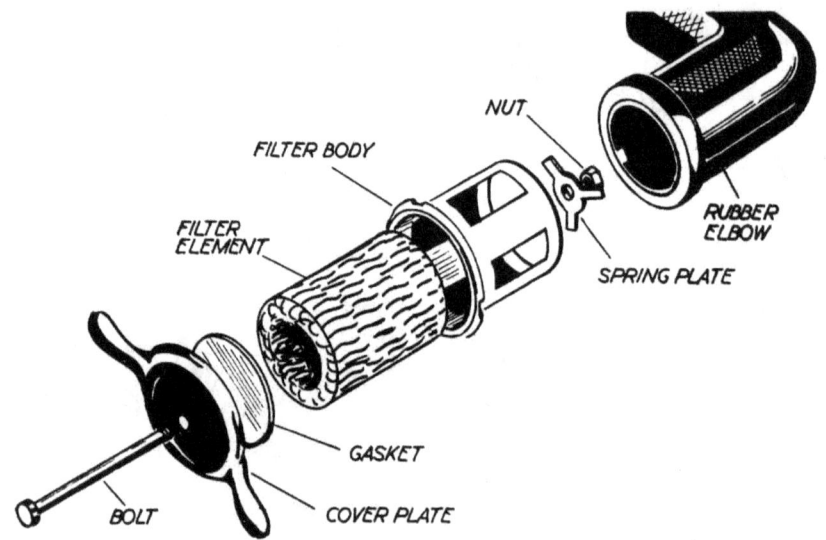

Fig. 41. Air Filter Quickly N, S, and L
This is mounted at bottom of frame and connected to carburettor with a rubber elbow.

indicates that the float has stuck. The lid of the float chamber and the float should be removed periodically and the float chamber washed but with petrol clean of any sediment which may have gathered in the bottom.

6a. CARBURETTOR QUICKLY-S/2 (and other three-speed models)
The carburettor in this instance is a Bing I/12/127—*see* Fig. 40A. This carburettor is generally similar to that on the two-speed engines but does, in fact, have a different body and throttle slide and cover. The main distinguishing feature is the very much thicker gasket mounted on the intake flange. The hose and air filter are also different and not interchangeable with the N, S, or L carburettor. Main details—main jet

DETAILED MAINTENANCE

size, 66; needle jet, 2·12; needle position, 2nd notch. Later models may have slightly different (larger) jet sizes.

On the S/2 23 and F models the carburettor is the Bing 1/12/136. a detailed illustration of which is shown in Fig. 40B. The main jet size with this carburettor is 64; needle jet 2·13; needle position, 2nd notch.

7. MAGNETO/GENERATOR

Only the 17-watt magneto-generator unit is scheduled for export models of the Quickly. The flywheel is exposed by removing the right-hand cover and can be rotated by hand to uncover the contact-breaker unit for access to the points for checking the gap and adjusting. (*See* Fig. 42.)

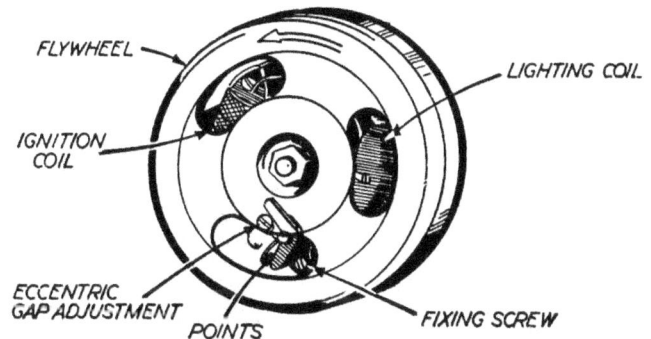

FIG. 42. ACCESS TO THE CONTACT BREAKER
This is achieved through one of the cut-outs in the flywheel. Points may be adjusted without removing the flywheel.

The normal contact gap is 0·008 to 0·012 in. (0·2–0·3 mm) and this can be checked with feeler gauges, turning over the engine by means of a pedal until the points are in the fully-open position. Adjustment of the points gap is made by engaging the eccentric adjuster with a screwdriver and turning. The points may also be cleaned and refaced, if necessary, through one of the flywheel openings, using a thin flat file with very fine teeth. Both contact faces should be perfectly flat and smooth and should contact each other over the whole of their surface, not at an angle touching at one edge. For better access to the contact breaker the flywheel can be removed.

It is necessary to use an extractor for this job, there being several patterns available. Depending on the type of extractor used the flywheel retaining nut is either unscrewed level with the outside of the flywheel, or removed entirely and replaced with a special cap or threaded bush. The extractor is then applied against the nut, cap or bush, the flywheel being held by the holder. An extractor should *never* be applied directly to the end of the crankshaft as this will almost invariably result in spreading of the thread. The flywheel is locked on to the crankshaft with a Woodruff key and so can only be reassembled in the same position as before. Care should be taken not to lose the key during the removing operation.

The stator or magneto backplate can be removed from the engine unit by unscrewing the two cheesehead screws on the backplate and the cheesehead screw on the terminal plate. The essential components mounted on the stator consist of the ignition coil, lighting coil, condenser, contact-breaker assembly and a lubricating pad for the shaft cam. (*See* Fig. 43.)

The magneto-generator unit may differ in small detail according to

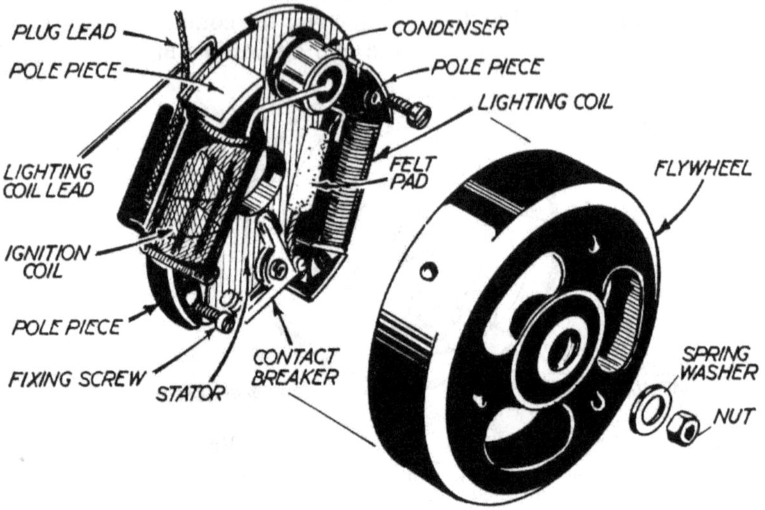

FIG. 43. THE FLYWHEEL MAGNETO-GENERATOR IN DETAIL
Standard unit is a Bosch LMUP L 2 on earlier models; Bosch LM UPA or Noris ELZJ alternative on later models.

model number, although many parts are common. Models prior to number 358 398/377 954 have the Bosch LMUP 1/115/17 L 2 unit with an inside flywheel diameter of 90·5 mm. The Bosch LM UPA unit fitted to subsequent models has an inside flywheel diameter of 85·5 mm, different stator, lighting and ignition coils, but the same rocker arm and condenser. Also specified is the Noris ELZJ 17/4 magneto-generator with many dissimilar parts again, although outwardly the same in general appearance. It is therefore important to specify the magneto type number when ordering spares.

Timing adjustment can be made, where necessary, by slackening the two cheeseheaded screws in the slotted holes in the stator and rotating the stator relative to the engine unit, bearing in mind that the engine rotates anticlockwise (viewed from the magneto end of the shaft). Thus rotating the stator clockwise will advance the spark, and anti-clockwise retard the spark. Only a very limited movement is possible, the correct

DETAILED MAINTENANCE 73

timing for the spark to occur (i.e. points open) is when the piston is 0·084 in. (2·1 mm) before top dead centre.

The timing position can be checked, if necessary, by removing the cylinder head, putting sleeves on two of the studs and tightening the cylinder temporarily with two nuts on these studs. The engine can then be turned over and the piston position measured with a depth gauge, related to contact-breaker movement.

Normally the only attention required by the magneto is a periodic application of grease to the felt lubricating pad which rubs against the cam-shaped section of the crankshaft (*see* Lubrication Table), and checking and adjustment of the contact-breaker gap and cleaning the points as a matter of routine maintenance.

Any electrical faults which may develop are generally obscure to the non-specialist and normally call for professional attention. It is as well to check first, however, that an apparent ignition or lighting coil failure is not in fact due to broken, frayed or disconnected leads, this type of fault being far more common than actual failure of the magneto-generator itself.

8. ENGINE UNIT

An exploded view of the complete engine unit is shown in Figs. 44 and 45. This is the same for all models, except that the spacer tube fitted on the bolts holding the right-hand engine cover and left-hand chain cover have been eliminated on later models and the gearbox mainshaft has been modified on models later than 20 964/21 026. The shape of the chain cover also differs on the N and S and L models.

If the engine is to be stripped it is first removed from the frame when its size and weight is such that it can easily be lifted and handled on a bench, or mounted on a special clamping fixture. (*See* Appendix IV.) This fixture is normally used with an assembly stand although for owner-servicing it is quite adequate to employ only the clamping fixture held in the jaws of a vice. The clamping fixture is not an indispensable piece of equipment for the complete operation of stripping and reassembly can readily be done with the engine laid on a suitable flat surface, such as a bench top. Recommended proportions for a stand to hold the machine upright whilst working on it are given in Fig. 46, although a conventional cycle stand of sturdy construction will do just as well.

To remove the engine, the chain cover is detached, the chain turned until the spring link comes in a convenient position, the spring link removed and the chain taken off. Also on this side the clutch cable is detached from the clutch lever.

The petrol tap is turned off, the rubber elbow between the carburettor and air intake pulled off and the carburettor and gasket removed by unscrewing the two hexagon nuts holding it to the cylinder.

The exhaust pipe and silencer is detached complete from the cylinder and frame. (*See* Section 10.)

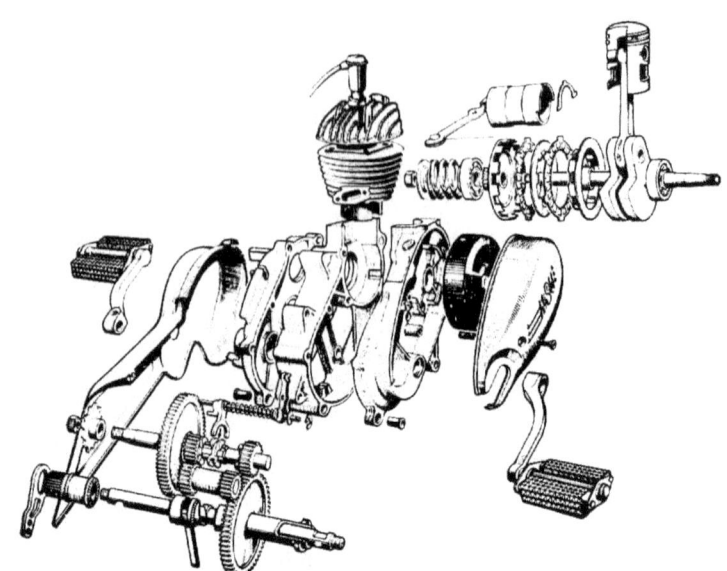

FIG. 44. DETAIL VIEW OF THE ENGINE UNIT, EXPLODED

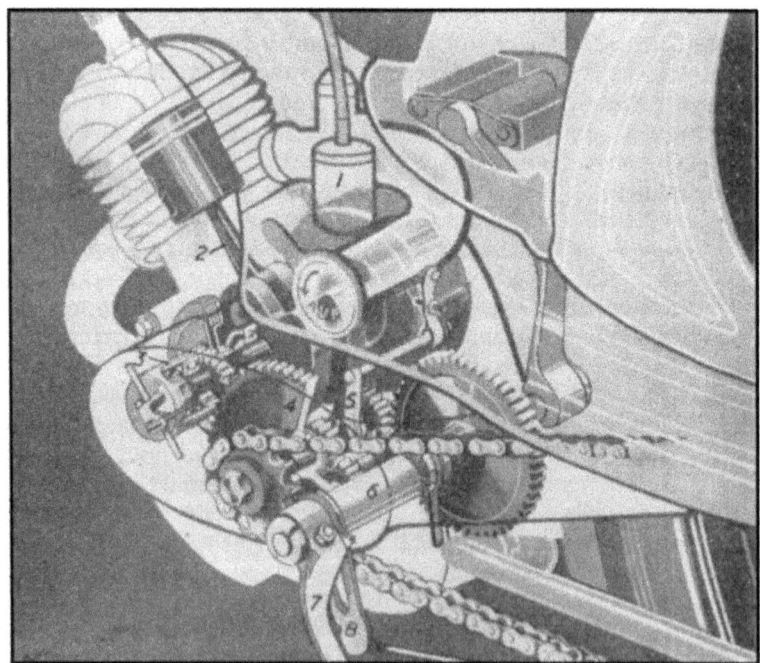

FIG. 45. CUT-AWAY DRAWING OF THE TWO-SPEED ENGINE UNIT

1 is the carburettor; 2 the piston-connecting rod-crankshaft assembly of the engine proper; 3 the clutch; 4 the main gear on the gearbox mainshaft; 5 the gear selector fork engaging the dog on the gearbox mainshaft (splined length); 6 the pedal crank spindle; 7 the pedal crank; and 8 the rear brake lever,

DETAILED MAINTENANCE

Disconnect the rear brake rod (or cable) from the brake arm. Remove the right-hand engine cover.

Withdraw the clutch cable through the slotted hole in the left-hand crankcase cover. Set the gearchange to second gear position, push the gearchange lever inwards and disconnect the cable, withdrawing this completely through the hole in the right-hand crankcase cover. The decompression valve cable is also released from the cylinder head.

The lighting lead is disconnected from the terminal on the magneto terminal plate and withdrawn upwards through the rubber sleeve.

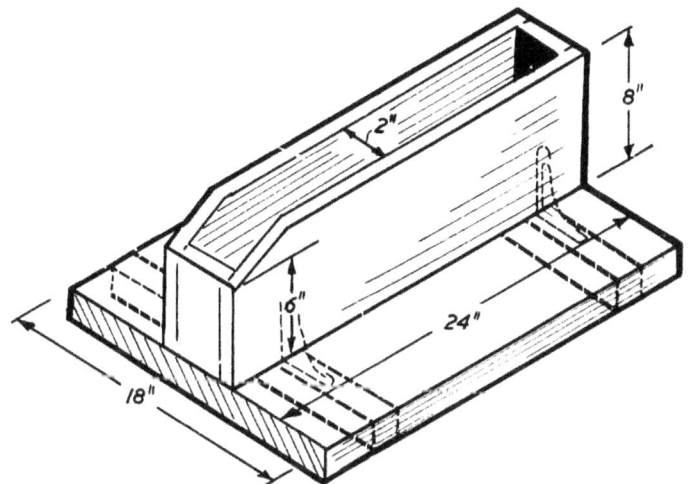

FIG. 46. FRONT WHEEL STAND

Details of a simple stand to hold the front wheel for maintenance work on engine, etc. Instead of a solid base, cross members may be fitted, attached with angle brackets (as shown dotted).

Finally, removing the three mounting bolts will enable the engine unit to be dropped out clear of the frame.

Stripping the Engine. (Refer to Figs. 47–50 for identification of parts.) Before attempting to strip the engine the outside should be cleaned off as much as possible with petrol or paraffin and a clean rag so that dirt and abrasive matter are not transferred to the inside, as well as to make the whole job less messy. Also, of course, before stripping the oil should be drained out of the crankcase by removing the drain plug in the left-hand crankcase cover and either the filler plug (right-hand side) or overflow screw (left-hand side).

The pedal cranks are removed by unscrewing the retaining nut on the end of the spindle and spring washer, and the nut and two washers retaining each cotter pin. The cotter pins can then be driven out with a light punch and the cranks and pedals pulled off the spindle.

The cylinder head is detached from the cylinder barrel by unscrewing the four nuts (first removing the plug lead and plug). The cylinder barrel then withdraws upwards. To remove the gudgeon pin the circlips at each end are taken off with pointed-nose pliers and the piston heated gently to a temperature a little above that of boiling water (approximately 250°F), when the gudgeon pin can be extracted with the gudgeon pin punch. (*See* Appendix IV.) The piston can then be laid aside and the lower cylinder gasket removed.

The engine is laid on its left side (or turned on the fixture until the right side is uppermost) to remove the flywheel (*see* Fig. 43) and stator plate (magneto backplate). The position of the stator can be marked to re-assemble without resetting the timing. The outer circlip and washer is also removed from the gearchange shaft.

Turning the engine the other way up the nut on the gearbox mainshaft is removed by locking the chain sprocket, e.g. with a screwdriver placed between the sprocket and clutch casing, and unscrewing. Remove the spring washer and withdraw the sprocket with an extractor. Remove the key from the shaft. A rubber sealing ring may be found fitted to the sprocket on earlier models. Detach the brake lever, which is retained by a circlip.

The small filler piece (*see* Appendix IV) should be stuck in the cotter pin groove in the pedal crank spindle with grease before attempting to remove the cover. This protects the rubber sealing rings in the brake sleeve immediately behind the cover and through which the spindle is withdrawn when the cover is lifted. The cover is held by seven nuts (with lock washers) and one bolt. If necessary to free after removing these nuts and bolt, it should be hit with a piece of wood or rubber hammer. Avoid hitting the cover with a hard tool, or on the edges, as otherwise the casting may fracture.

Once the cover plate is removed the brake sleeve may be detached from it by taking off the circlip. Also the crankcase gasket should be removed.

The clutch-operating cup can be levered off with a pair of screwdrivers or the special levers (*see* Appendix IV) after the spring clip is first pushed to one side off the cup. The nut on the crankshaft can then be unscrewed, holding the gear pinion against rotation with the special tool. (*See* Appendix IV.) Following the two spring washers the outer retaining cup, spring, inner retaining cup and ball race can be withdrawn. (*See* Fig. 50.)

The washer and pinion can now be withdrawn from the gearbox mainshaft, freeing as necessary by "jiggling" rather than using force. Follow by removing the clutch pinion and outer casing and the three clutch plates, withdrawn from the crankshaft. The inner clutch casing is released by removing the small circlip, the casing may then be prised free with the same levers used for extracting the clutch cup. There remains a rubber sealing ring on this side of the shaft which need not be removed until the crankshaft is taken out.

DETAILED MAINTENANCE

Working from the other side of the engine, unscrewing the centrally located nut and bolt enables the crankcase to be finally taken apart and the remaining components dismantled.

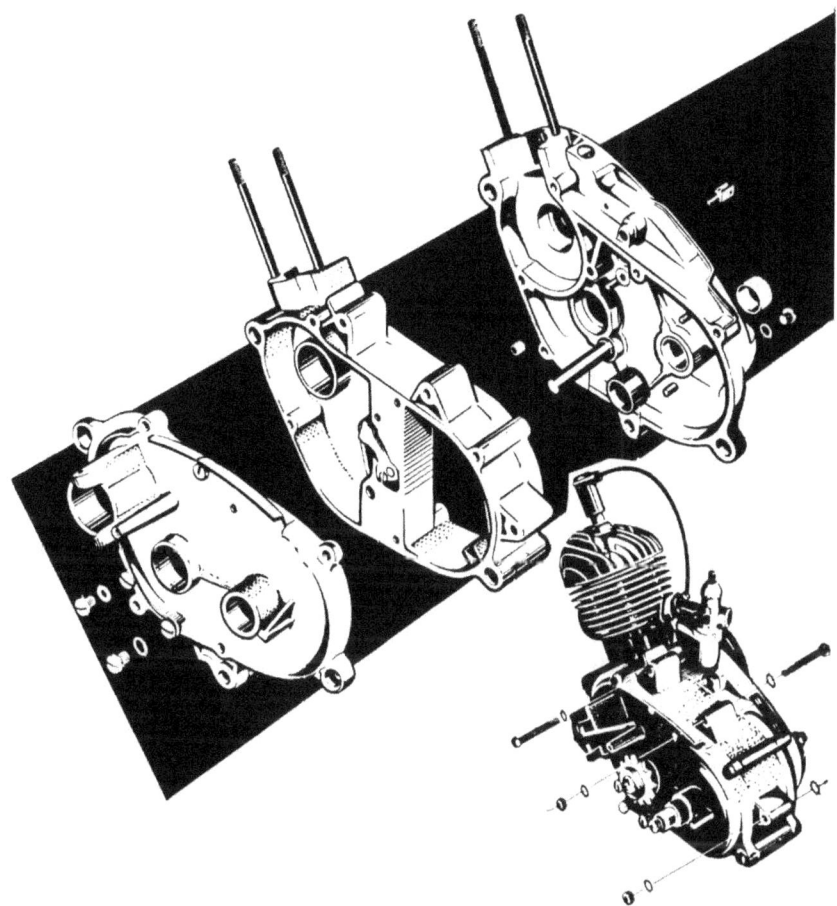

FIG. 47. CRANKCASE COMPONENTS ASSEMBLED AND EXPLODED

Three-speed Gearbox (Quickly-S/2, Cavallino, and T models). Details of the three-speed gearbox are shown in Fig. 49A. Stripping, etc., follows a similar procedure as that outlined for the two-speed gearbox. The following specific instructions apply as regards adjustment of gear-change. Any play on the Bowden cables is adjusted with the cable adjusters with first and third gear engaged. Aim for positive but smooth movement and check that all three gears are properly engaged. If the cables are tightened too much the gear-change will be hard to operate.

[*Contd. on p.* 81]

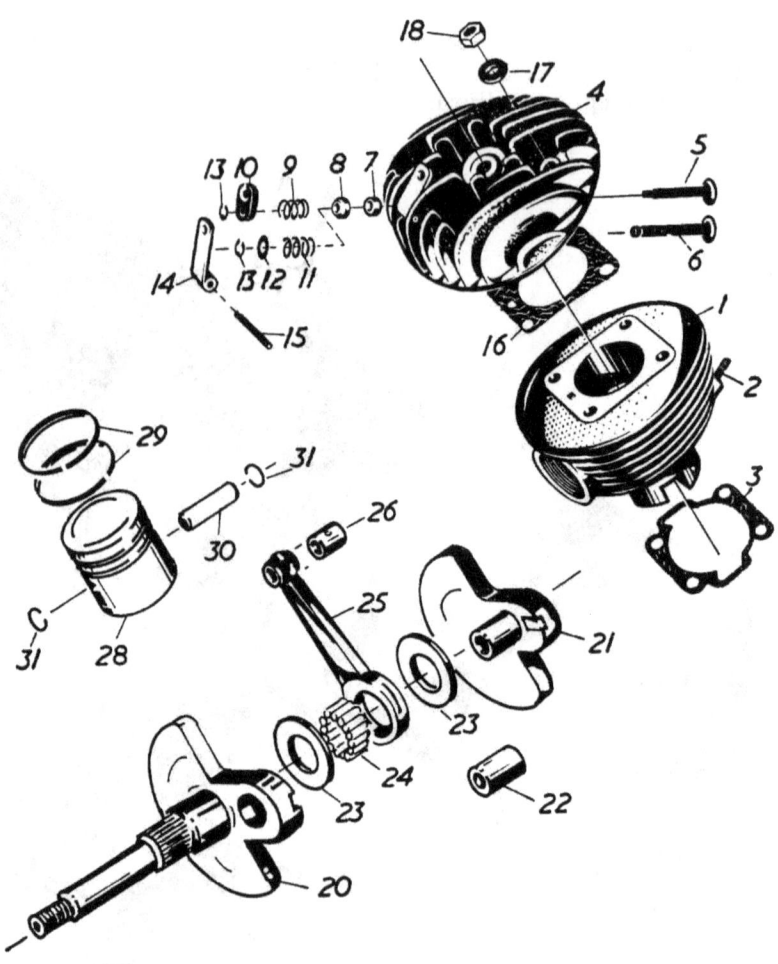

FIG. 48. COMPONENT PARTS OF THE QUICKLY ENGINE

1. Cylinder
2. Stud
3. Gasket (lower cylinder)
4. Cylinder head
5. Decompressor valve (early models)
6. Decompressor valve (late models)
7. Packing
8. Cap
9. Spring } early models
10. Thrust plate
11. Spring } late models
12. Washer
13. C-washer
14. Release lever } late models
15. Washer
16. Head gasket
17. Washer
18. Nut
20. Crankshaft half
21. Crankshaft half
22. Crankpin
23. Washer
24. Roller bearings (16)
25. Connecting rod
26. Bush
28. Piston
29. Piston rings
30. Gudgeon pin
31. Circlips

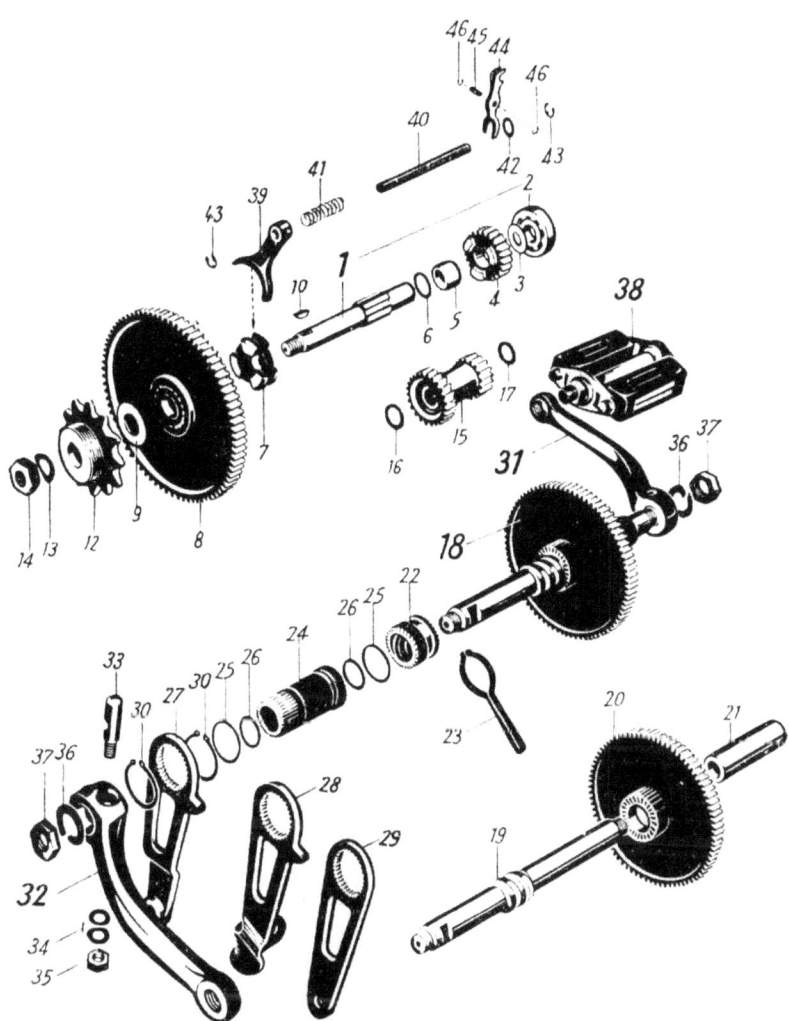

FIG. 49. GEARBOX AND PEDAL COMPONENTS, TWO-SPEED MODELS

1. Gearbox mainshaft
2. Bearing
3. Washer
4. Gear
5. Bush
6. Washer
7. Dog
8. Gear
9. Washer
10. Woodruff key
12. Sprocket
13. Spring washer
14. Nut
15. Gear
16. Washer
17. Washer
18. Crank axle unit
19. Crank spindle
20. Gear
21. Spacer
22. Driver
23. Spring
24. Locking member
25. Seal ring
26. Seal ring
27. Brake lever (early models)
28. Brake lever (late models)
29. Brake lever (L model)
30. Circlip
31. Right crank
32. Left crank
33. Screw wedge
34. Spring washer
35. Nut
36. Spring washer
37. Nut
38. Pedal
39. Selector fork
40. Striker shaft
41. Spring
42. Washer
43. C-washer
44. Striker lever
45. Pin ⎫ early models
46. C-washer ⎭

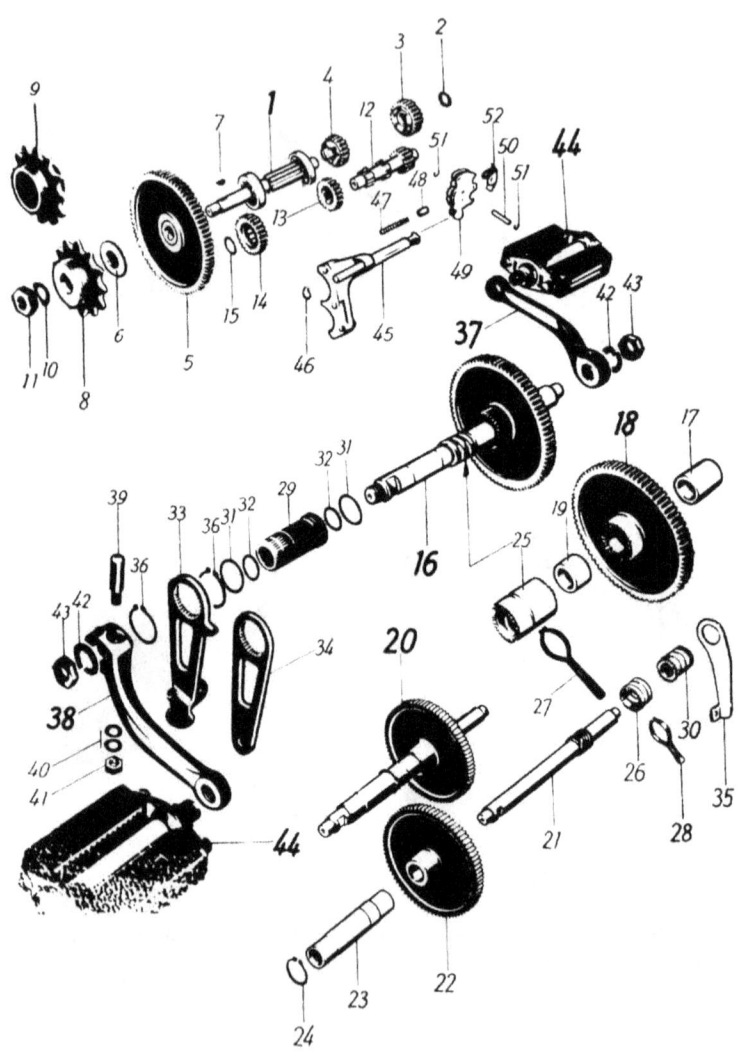

Fig. 49A. Three-speed Gearbox on Quickly-S/2 and F
(also Cavallino, T and TT Models)

DETAILED MAINTENANCE 81

Some gearchange troubles were experienced on the Quickly-T due to the fitting of faulty twistgrips with the curved tube not correctly tempered, requiring replacement of this tube and the fulcrum plates. This should not apply to later models.

Another trouble experienced on the earlier three-speed models was slipping in second gear. This can be overcome by adjusting the axial play of the layshaft to between 0·2 and 0·3 mm. Shims are available as standard spares for this purpose, ranging from 0·5 to 0·9 mm thickness in 0·1 mm steps.

Reassembly Procedure. For convenience of reference, reassembly of the engine is summarized under basic operations required in correct sequence, all parts being clean and lightly oiled before refitting. References to Figs. 47–50 will clarify the instructions.

1. Start on right-hand half crankcase with gearbox side facing upwards. Stick on gasket with jointing compound.
2. Fit crankshaft with or without shim washers on the right-hand shaft, according to play. (Play should not be more than 0·012 in.)
3. Assemble gearbox mainshaft and bottom gear pinion in crankcase half.
4. Insert gearchange spindle from the outside.
5. Fit gearchange selector fork (lugs downwards) and dogs, also spring. Fit circlip.
6. Mount pedal crank spindle and gear pinion in the crankshaft half.
7. Put thrust washer on gearbox mainshaft. Insert layshaft and fit thrust washer (1 mm thick or 2 mm thick, according to model number).
8. Place the two fitted sleeves in right-hand crankcase.
9. Coat edges of left crankcase with jointing compound and assemble

---

KEY TO FIG. 49A
Note: Many components are common with the N, S, and L unit. Principal differences are—

20–24. Crank axle assembly 30. Locking member
26. Driver 35. Brake operating lever
28. Spring 38, 39. Cranks

Compare also gearbox group (top) with Fig. 49 (two-speed gearbox)
Key to other items—

1. Main shaft
2. Washer
3. 25-tooth gear
4. 17-tooth gear
5. 16/80-tooth gear
6. Shim
7. Key
8. 12-tooth sprocket
9. 13-tooth sprocket (optional)
10. Spring washer
11. Nut
12. Main shaft, 16 teeth
13. 17-tooth gear
14. 25-tooth gear
15. Washer
16–19. Crank axle assembly N, S, and L
20–24. Crank axle assembly S/2
25. Driver N, S and L
26. Driver S/2
27. Spring N, S, and L
28. Spring S/2
29. Locking member N, S, and L
30. Locking member S/2
31, 32. Seal ring
34. Brake lever, N, S, and Cavallino
35. Brake lever, T, TT, and S/2
45. Selector fork

on top of right crankcase, holding with the bolt passed from left to right through the assembly. One star washer goes under the head of the bolt and one under the nut. This bolt must not be tightened up excessively otherwise the crankcase will be distorted. Place driver and sliding spring on pedal crank spindle, narrow end facing the pinion. Locate spring eye in recess in left-hand crankcase.

10. Fit rubber sealing ring to crankcase.

11. Fit inner clutch casing and circlip, pushing the casing in place with the special tool.

12. Assemble clutch plates in order and fit outer clutch casing.

13. Assemble the gear pinion on the gearbox mainshaft.

14. Assemble ball race and inner cup, clutch spring and outer cup on the crankshaft. Use the special tool to compress the spring and fit the two spring washers and nut, using a holder on the gear pinion to lock the shaft. The nut should be tightened up until the clutch slips.

15. Fit clutch cup and push the circlip in place. The lugs may be bent to ensure that the circlip is seated properly.

16. Push brake sleeve into left-hand crankcase cover.

17. Stick gasket to left-hand crankcase cover with jointing compound.

18. Fit tapered sleeve in cover and filler piece to pedal crank spindle.

19. Fit left-hand crankcase cover carefully (fitted sleeves in position) and secure with the seven nuts and two lock washers on each stud and the long bolt, nut and two lock washers—the nut on the right-hand side of the crankcase.

20. Fit the circlip retaining the brake sleeve and attach the brake lever in the correct attitude with its circlip.

21. Assemble spring washer, chain sprocket, spring washer and nut on the gearbox mainshaft and tighten up. (On earlier models the sprocket is followed by a rubber sealing ring and two spring washers.)

22. Working on the right-hand side of the engine, place the washer and circlip on the gearchange spindle and check the action.

23. Fit magneto backplate and ignition lead and reattach terminal plate to crankcase.

24. Fit and tighten flywheel, locating in position on the shaft with the Woodruff key and holding the flywheel with a holder to tighten.

25. Fit lower cylinder gasket.

26. Insert one circlip in piston, and assemble on connecting rod little end by pushing gudgeon pin in place (it should not be necessary to warm the piston). Lock with the second circlip. Check that the piston is the right way round—the longer edge of the port facing the rear of the engine.

27. Pull the piston up as far as it will go and insert two strips of wood under the bottom to act as supports. Grip the piston with piston ring pliers to close the rings and slide on the cylinder carefully, finally removing the wooden strips to allow the bottom of the cylinder to seat against the gasket.

DETAILED MAINTENANCE 83

28. Fit cylinder head gasket, checking that it is the right way round (i.e. passage from decompressor valve to exhaust is open).
29. Add head gasket and fit head, tightening down with the four nuts.
30. Fit the right-hand pedal crank first, securing with the cotter pin and then the retaining nut. Under no circumstances should the engine be

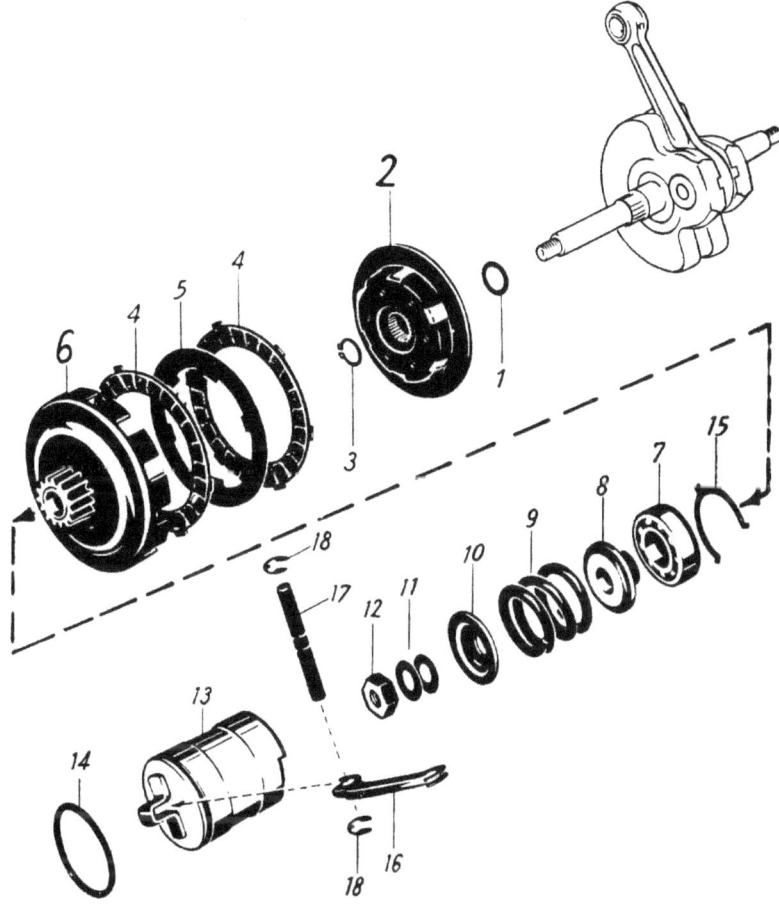

Fig. 50. The Clutch Detailed

1. Seal ring
2. Inner housing
3. Circlip
4. Clutch plate
5. Clutch plate
6. Clutch housing and pinion
7. Bearing
8. Inner retailer
9. Spring
10. Outer retainer
11. Spring washer
12. Nut
13. Clutch bell (cup)
14. Seal ring
15. C-washer
16. Clutch lever
17. Spindle
18. C-washer

turned over with one pedal not fitted as this will tend to force the pedal crank spindle bush out of position and necessitate stripping the engine again to replace.

31. Fit left-hand pedal crank. Note that the pedals are distinguished with marks "L" for left hand and "R" for right hand and, if the pedal itself is to be unscrewed from the crank, the left-hand pedal has a left-hand thread and the right-hand pedal a right-hand thread.

9. REPLACEMENT OF ENGINE PARTS

Owing to the nature of the construction employed (chrome plated light alloy), the cylinder cannot be "rebored" when worn, as with most conventional engines. When wear has become excessive, in fact, the only solution is a replacement cylinder-and-piston set. It is essential to obtain a matched set, matching being done by selective assembly from a graduated range of pistons and cylinders manufactured within specified dimensional limits. These limits are too wide for "random" fitting; for example, a piston which happened to be the smallest possible size within the manufacturing specification would be too "sloppy" a fit in a cylinder which happened to have the largest possible bore—again within the manufacturing specification. For the purpose of selection, therefore, pistons and cylinders as made are graded in sizes differing in appreciably less than one-thousandth of an inch in diameter, and matched components are taken from the same grade size.

The original manufacturing tolerances are themselves quite small but the complete range is covered in ten different steps or grade sizes. These numbers are scribed on both the pistons and cylinders (1 to 10) and similar numbers therefore appear on a matched set. The question of specifying similar gradation numbers for piston and cylinder does not arise in purchasing replacements for this is always done in the initial selection by the manufacturers.

There are two patterns of cylinder head, differing only with respect to the decompressor valve assembly. It is quite practicable, if required, to refit the later pattern head to earlier models, should a replacement be necessary. The compression ratio of the engine, and with it the performance, can be increased slightly by omitting the head gasket, although this is certainly not to be recommended as general practice for the mating faces of the head and cylinder may be damaged by burning as a consequence. It is, however, the simplest method of getting a little extra out of the engine for *apparently* nothing.

The crankshaft assembly—or as specified by NSU, the flywheel assembly—is available only as a complete replacement unit, including also the main bearings. Thus it is not possible to replace, say, only the connecting rod in an existing assembly to cure "big end" knock. Actually the amount of "knock" through wear which can be tolerated is often a matter of the owner's attitude to a working piece of machinery. Some

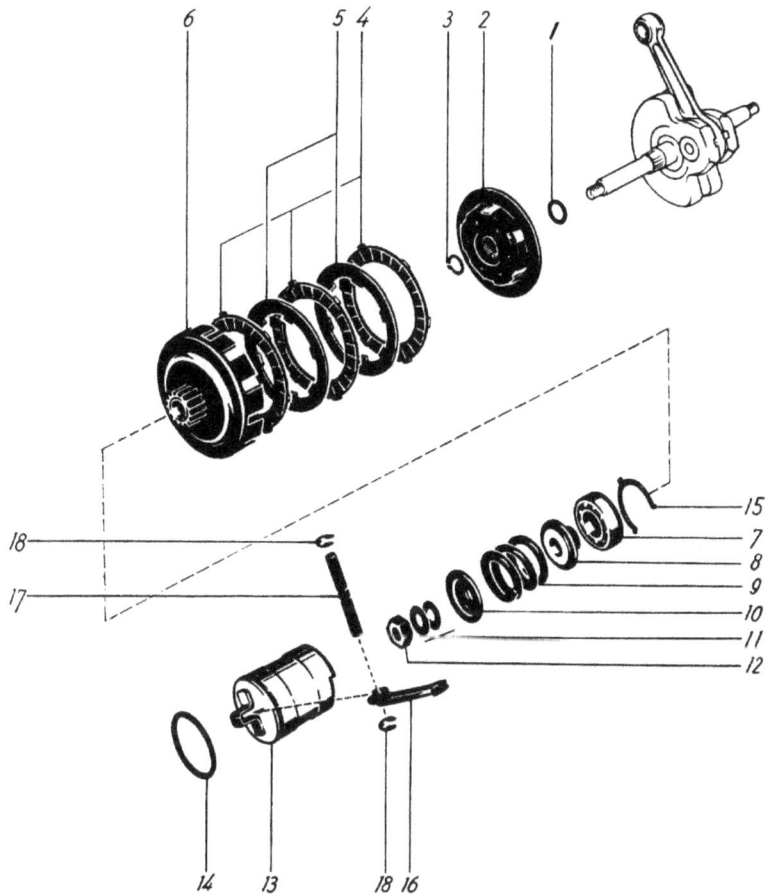

FIG. 50A. THE FIVE-PLATE CLUTCH AS USED ON QUICKLY 23 MODELS N, S, S/2 AND F

1. Seal ring
2. Inner body
3. Circlip
4. Clutch plate
5. Clutch plate
6. Clutch outer housing
7. Grooved bearing
8. Spring retainer, inner
9. Clutch spring
10. Spring retainer, outer
11. Spring washer
12. Nut
13. Clutch cup
14. Gasket
15. Circlip
16. Clutch lever
17. Spindle
18. Circlip

people rush for replacements at the first indications of wear being present. Others happily carry on for thousands of miles, probably in blissful ignorance that a part of the engine unit has developed appreciable wear through long use. In point of fact the amount of wear the Quickly crankshaft will tolerate without giving trouble is considerable and normal wear is only to be expected after a working life of thousands of miles and millions of firing strokes hammering on the piston. A rapid rate of wear can, however, result from mis-handling of the machine, particularly as regards lack of attention to lubrication. Cutting down on the proportion of oil specified for the petrol-oil mixture as an "economy" measure is asking for trouble—and a heavy repair bill at an early date.

When reassembling an engine which has been stripped, the amount of axial play in the crankshaft assembly can be measured and taken up to within a specified limit by adding plain washers to the right-hand side of the crankshaft. Crankshaft clearance can be measured in each half of the crankcase using a depth gauge across the edges. The sum of these two dimensions (i.e. the clearance in each half crankcase) less the dimension across the crankshaft webs gives the axial play. This should not exceed 0·012 in. (0·3 mm). Washer thicknesses are chosen to reduce axial play within this limit.

Another important point to watch in reassembling an engine is that the piston is refitted the correct way round, i.e. with the longer edge of the port facing towards the *rear*. If this is not so the gas passages will not interconnect properly and so the engine will not run. Care should also be taken when replacing the cylinder to see that the bottom of the piston is properly supported as the cylinder is slid in place—not forced—down the studs. Ignition timing can be checked at this stage—as described elsewhere (Section 7)—by fitting short sleeves over to the studs so that the nuts can be screwed down to clamp the cylinder securely without the head in place.

It is particularly important with all engine replacements parts that only genuine Quickly spares be used, more particularly as these are of metric rather than English sizes. As a guide to when modifications have affected engine—and other component—spares, details of model changes are listed in Appendix II. On current models the magneto-generator may be of either Bosch or Noris manufacture, virtually identical in appearance but differing in detail parts specification. The particular manufacturer's name is embossed on both the rotor and stator assemblies of each unit as a quick means of identification. Alternatively quoting the engine number should be sufficient for spares identification purposes.

10. DECARBONIZING

Decarbonizing of the silencer and cylinder head is recommended every 1,200–1,500 miles, or whenever the need is apparent through a falling-off

DETAILED MAINTENANCE

in power from the engine. Decarbonizing the cylinder itself may be delayed for some 4,000 to 6,000 miles, depending largely on how the machine is driven. The best indication that the cylinder could do with decarbonizing is that the falling-off in power is not rectified by decarbonizing the head and silencer only.

The job of decarbonizing the cylinder head and silencer is very simple. Decarbonizing the cylinder involves lifting the cylinder barrel off the engine and many owners may prefer to have this job done for them by a local service station, although again it is not a particularly skilled job.

The silencer fitted may be one of several types—all virtually the same in external appearance but differing in construction. If there is a small screw

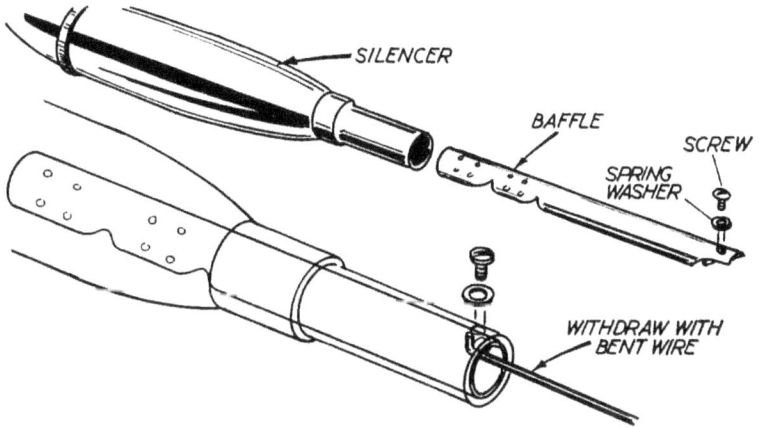

FIG. 51. REMOVAL OF BAFFLE TUBE

The baffle tube on the silencer can be withdrawn for decarbonizing with a piece of bent wire (some models). Other models may have differently assembled silencer unit.

near the end of the tailpipe this can be removed to release the exhaust pipe baffle which can then be withdrawn for cleaning with the aid of a piece of stiff wire bent over at right angles at the end. (*See* Fig. 51.) Alternatively the baffle section may be held with a spring clip inside the end of the tailpipe; or the silencer body is in two halves and may be drawn apart by unscrewing the small nut visible in the end of the tailpipe. Once dismantled the baffle tube can be decarbonized by scraping off all the sooty deposit which has accumulated around it, and inside the tube. It should then be reassembled complete as before.

If the silencer and exhaust pipe complete are to be removed from the machine, slacken the clip and bolt on the frame holding the silencer and unscrew the large slotted nut holding the end of the exhaust pipe in the cylinder with a C-spanner. The complete unit can then be removed.

The cylinder head is easily removed for decarbonizing by detaching the plug lead and the decompression valve cable (*see* Section 1) and then the four nuts and washers holding the head down. The head can then be lifted off and the hemispherical-shaped combustion chamber scraped clean of carbon with a piece of wood or similar soft scraper (not metal) after first removing the plug.

When the head is removed it is generally good practice to reface the decompression valve seating by re-grinding. The valve is released by springing off the C-washer on the end of the stem. Then it may be withdrawn inwards. The small components released comprise a thrust plate, spring, cap and packing in the case of machines up to serial number 482 754/522 989. On subsequent machines a washer replaces the thrust plate, and the head incorporates a release lever mounted on a pin. The valves are also different in the length of stem. (*See* Fig. 48.)

Re-grinding is done merely by coating the valve face with grinding paste and rotating the valve against its seating under pressure. It is unlikely that the seating will need much re-grinding if this operation is done regularly (e.g. whenever the head is removed for decarbonizing) but the seating may be damaged, and the valve itself burnt, if the decompression control is wrongly used, for instance if used frequently in place of the throttle.

Before replacing the head, examine the head gasket for possible damage and, if in doubt as to its condition, replace with a new one. Check that the gasket is refitted the right way round. The laminated aluminium gaskets standard on later models should seldom need replacing.

To remove the cylinder for decarbonizing, remove the head first, then the gasket and lift the cylinder straight off, covering the opening in the crankcase with a clean cloth as you do so, to prevent any dirt from falling in. After scraping off all carbon with a wooden scraper or similar tool, replace carefully in the same position, squeezing in the piston rings one at a time by hand to let the piston enter the bottom of the cylinder. A light smearing of oil on the inside of the cylinder is recommended before reassembly rather than fitting back dry. The operation of removing and refitting the cylinder can, of course, also be carried out with the engine still mounted on the frame, only in this case the silencer fitting will have to be slackened-off and the exhaust pipe detached from the cylinder first.

In general it is best to delay decarbonizing of the cylinder for as long as possible and so leave the piston rings undisturbed. When the cylinder unit is removed for decarbonizing, the piston top should be similarly scraped clean of carbon and it may also appear advisable to remove the piston rings and clean out the ring grooves. It is not, however, necessary to detach the piston from the connecting rod for this purpose. A broken or obviously worn ring would, of course, be replaced but if both rings are in good condition they should preferably be replaced in the same order as before and the same way up.

11. SOURCES OF TROUBLE

The NSU Quickly properly driven and properly maintained, enjoys the reputation of being particularly trouble-free. Experience of the NSU Maintenance Establishment has, however, shown the following to be sources of trouble.

Engine Vibrating Loose. The importance of checking engine holding bolts at regular *weekly* intervals has been stressed earlier on. If the engine does work loose and is allowed to continue running in this condition, permanent damage to the frame holes can result. It is essential that, if the engine bolts are removed, the star washers be replaced both under the heads of the bolts and behind the nuts. On later models the star washers under the heads of the two bolts holding the carrying handle have been replaced by locking plates and it is a wise precaution to replace with these in any case on machines which are not so fitted.

Water in the Carburettor. This is a not unknown occurrence on earlier models. Later models have a small hole drilled in the frame to drain off water which might otherwise get into the carburettor.

Water in the Magneto. When the small insulating flap at the end of the high-tension lead becomes worn there is the possibility of water seeping through into the magneto and shorting out the high tension, so that there is no spark. This can be cured by the fitting of a new flap or the use of Bostik compound to repair the damage and renew the seal. Temporarily, a covering of Plasticine will act as a suitable seal.

Shorting Rear Lamp. This canc ocur when the terminal block in the headlamp becomes badly worn or damaged, or the dipswitch has worn to the point of becoming faulty. This fault can be quite obscure if the wire only is suspected.

Look for the Easy Way. Many owners make a long job of what should be a simple replacement—taking down half the engine to replace a clutch cable, for example. The answer to this is to become quite familiar with the various techniques discussed in this chapter so that any particular job of maintenance can be done the easiest—and most direct—way.

6 Electrical Equipment

THE electricity for the spark plug and for the lights and horn is generated by the flywheel magneto-dynamo, hidden under the flywheel. Although this is a single unit it consists, essentially, of a magneto supplying the sparking current to the spark plug, and a separate form of "dynamo" or electricity generator supplying the lights and horn.

PRINCIPLE OF OPERATION

The principle of operation can be followed with reference to Fig. 52. On a circular backplate or stator are two coils terminating in soft iron pole pieces closely matching the shape of the flywheel rim which rotates around them. To the flywheel rim are attached four permanent magnets. The backplate or stator is fixed and the flywheel is driven by the engine crankshaft, so that when the flywheel is in position these magnets fitted to the flywheel rim just clear the coil pole pieces during rotation.

Each time a magnet passes one of the pole pieces its magnetic field produces a reaction in the coil, generating a surge of electricity in the coil, first in one direction and then the other. Since there are four rim magnets, this effect will be experienced by each coil four times per revolution.

Dynamo Circuit. In the case of the lighting coil there is a continuous generation of *alternating* current at a frequency *four* times that of the engine speed, all the time the engine is running. Thus if the lighting coil is connected up to the lights and horn, inserting switches as controls, these form complete electrical circuits. Rather than connect both sides of the lighting coil up with wires to these external circuits, one side of the coil is "earthed" or connected directly to the backplate, leaving only a single wire to be connected to the main circuits. The lamps and horn are similarly earthed (i.e. one side connected to a metal part of the frame, which is obviously in electrical contact with the metal backplate to which the other lighting coil end is connected).

Since both the amount and frequency of current generated by the lighting coil is dependent on engine r.p.m., the lights will be relatively dim at low speed and the horn low-pitched; and vice versa at high speed. The difference in horn note, in fact, is particularly noticeable.

Magneto Circuit. The magneto side is slightly more complicated. The same sort (and frequency) of current is generated in the magneto coil

ELECTRICAL EQUIPMENT

but since we require only one spark per revolution at the spark plug, only one current surge per revolution is utilized. Also the coil is not a single coil but a double winding, consisting of a primary coil with a relatively small number of turns over which is wound a secondary coil of thinner wire and many more turns.

To get the necessary high tension output for the spark to jump the gap between the spark plug electrodes—and also to make this spark occur at the proper time—a pair of contacts or "points" is inserted in the primary circuit which, when opened, cause a very rapid change of current in the

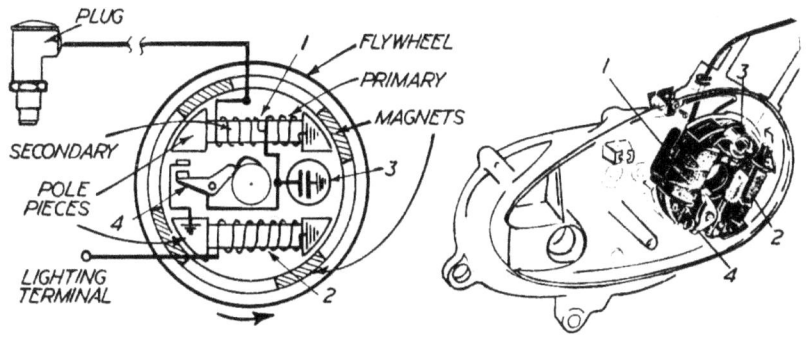

Fig. 52. A Magneto Circuit

A typical magneto circuit is shown, together with an *in situ* view of the Quickly magneto: 1 is the ignition coil; 2 the lighting coil; 3 the condenser; and 4 the contact-breaker.

primary. This surge is transformed, by mutual inductance between the two coils wound on top of each other, into a surge of *high-voltage* electricity in the secondary coil. The secondary coil is connected to the spark plug central electrode and is sufficiently high to jump the gap to the other electrode on the body of the plug, earthed by being screwed into the cylinder head. The other side of the secondary coil is earthed to complete the return circuit. (*See* Fig. 52.)

Make-and-break Mechanism. The "make and break" of the contact points is governed by a cam fitted on the engine crankshaft, closing and then opening the points abruptly once each revolution by working against a pivoted fibre plate of special shape (the contact-breaker). One of the points is mounted on the contact-breaker and the other, adjacent to it, is fixed and mounted on the backplate. Quite obviously the moment of opening of the points depends on the relative mounting positions of the contact-breaker and crankshaft cam, and the layout is designed to produce opening at the right time (i.e. 2·1 mm or 0·084 in. before the piston reaches its uppermost or top dead-centre position in the cylinder). Actually the "timing" is not completely fixed by the design layout. Provision is made for the backplate to be slackened-off and rotated a small amount either way to adjust the timing, as necessary. It is also necessary to ensure that current is being generated in the magneto coil at the instant the points open, i.e. that one of the rim magnets is passing the pole piece of the coil, but this is not critical. Provided the magnet is near enough in position—and there are four of them quite closely spaced—the magnetic field of one will be effective. So, in whatever position the flywheel is bolted on to the crankshaft, the magneto coil will remain effective as a spark generator. The correct position, however (i.e. the one corresponding to maximum effect), is when the break gap of the pole shoe is between $\frac{3}{8}$–$\frac{1}{2}$ in. The direction of rotation of the flywheel is shown by an arrow.

One more component is included in the electrical circuit—a condenser which is virtually connected across the points. This assists in the proper generation of the high-voltage surge in the secondary and also acts as a spark quench across the points to prevent them arcing and thus becoming pitted or burnt. It is a component which is not heavily loaded and should never normally give any trouble. Normally, in fact, the only maintenance required on the magneto unit is a periodic check of the contact-breaker gap and readjustment, if necessary, and cleaning of the points if pitted or burnt. Further details of this are described in Chapter 5, Section 7.

THE SPARKING PLUG

A Bosch type W 240 T 11 spark plug is fitted as standard on all Quickly engines, this type also being available from NSU agents as a replacement item. The British equivalent is the KLG F80, which can be used as an alternative. It is a good idea always to carry a spare *clean* plug in the tool-box as the plug is the first component to suspect in the event of the engine stopping, or running badly. Operating in an atmosphere of petrol and oil which burns at a high temperature, all spark plugs are prone to soot up or become covered with a carbon deposit. This does not normally interfere with their operation unless the carboning-up is severe, but it is quite possible that a "whisker" of carbon can form between the plug electrodes, effectively shorting them out so that no spark occurs. Such a plug will normally be quite all right again, once cleaned, but the opportunity should also be taken to check the gap between the electrodes (*see* Fig. 21) and readjust, if necessary.

The operation of a spark plug can readily be checked by removing it, then replacing the high-tension lead and holding the body of the plug against the engine, holding the lead and not the plug (otherwise you will get a strong shock). If the engine is then turned over, a strong spark should appear across the electrodes corresponding to each revolution of the engine.

This is no automatic guarantee that the plug will spark satisfactorily inside the engine when reassembled, for under compression the electrode gap is effectively some eight to ten times greater than in air. Thus, for

ELECTRICAL EQUIPMENT

enough voltage to jump 0·020 in. under compression, the corresponding "free air" gap will be a matter of $\frac{3}{16}$ in. or more. The quality of the spark delivered by the magneto coil can be checked by leaving the plug in the engine but disconnecting the high-tension lead and holding it about $\frac{3}{16}$–$\frac{1}{4}$ in. away from the top of the plug, or a convenient point on the engine. Turning the engine over should produce a spark jumping this gap with an audible crack. If so, there is certainly enough voltage to bridge the spark plug electrode gap (if normal) and if the plug is failing it is almost certainly because it is excessively dirty, or perhaps faulty (e.g. cracked insulator). Changing the spark plug, or cleaning the plug if dirty, should produce an immediate cure.

For correct operation the spark for igniting the fuel mixture must be of the right temperature. If the electrodes are too "cold" they will allow oil to collect on the points and foul them. Any liquid collecting on the electrodes will normally tend to prevent the spark from forming, which is the main reason why a flooded engine will not start. If the plug points remain too hot, then they may ignite the fuel before the correct time, i.e. before the spark occurs. All these features are bound up in the engine design, and that is why the specified type of plug usually gives best results and alternative plugs of a "hotter" or "colder" type may give troublesome running.

The actual mixture drawn in by the engine also affects the operation of the plug. A correctly balanced plug will soot up but the deposit will be a uniform grey in appearance. If the electrodes are white and heavily corroded then the plug is too "soft" for the mixture. Conversely, if the deposit on the electrodes and up inside the plug around the insulator is very black and oily in appearance the plug is too "hard." Before condemning the plug, if a standard or recommended type, check that you are using the right petrol-oil mixture and then the carburettor settings. (*See* Chapter 5, Section 6.)

LIGHTS AND LIGHTING CIRCUIT

A complete wiring diagram appropriate to the Quickly-N and Quickly-S is shown in Fig. 53, the various leads being identified by colour coding, as listed. Wiring on the Quickly-L is slightly different. (*See* Fig. 54.) Both these circuits apply to the standard export models with 6-volt, 17-watt, lighting coil output. The wiring circuit appropriate to earlier models with a 6-volt, 3-watt system is shown in Fig. 55. Very little trouble should be experienced with the lighting circuit, apart from the possibility of broken or frayed leads (giving an intermittent earth through contact with part of the frame) and a broken filament in the headlight or tail-lamp bulb. Replacement bulbs, when fitted, should always be of the recommended voltage and wattage, viz.—

Headlight (all models) 6-volt, 15/15-watt (double filament).
Tail-lamp (all models) 6-volt, 2-watt.

94   THE BOOK OF THE NSU QUICKLY

The headlamp beam can readily be adjusted, if necessary. The best setting for night driving is for the centre of the beam to fall on the ground

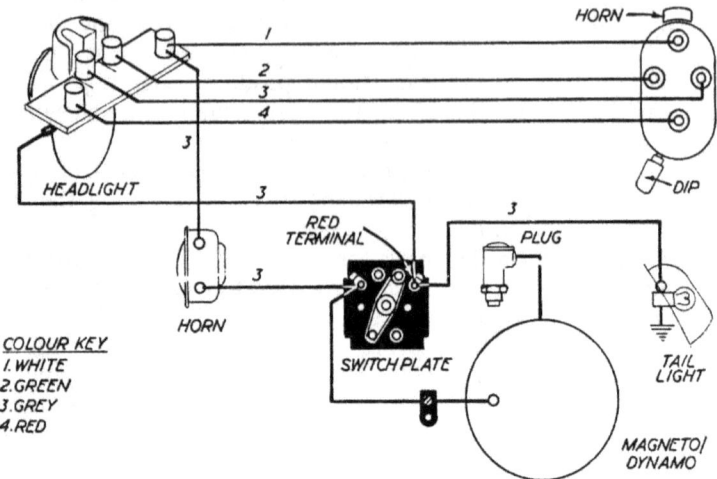

FIG. 53. WIRING DIAGRAM FOR QUICKLY-N, -S AND S/2 MODELS

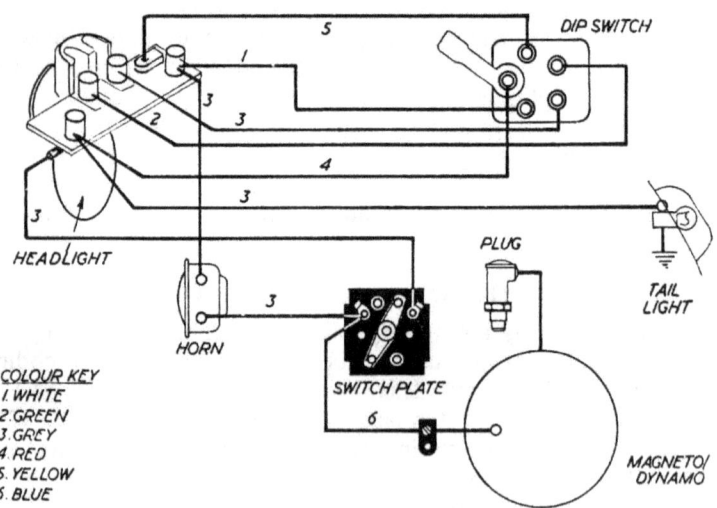

FIG. 54. WIRING DIAGRAM FOR QUICKLY-L MODEL

about 30–35 ft in front of the machine (i.e. ten to twelve paces) when sitting astride the machine on level ground. To adjust the headlamp on the Quickly-N and Quickly-S, loosen the hexagon-headed screw at the back and realign the lamp as required before tightening up again. On the

ELECTRICAL EQUIPMENT

Quickly-L the headlamp housing is integral with the handlebars, and adjustment of the beam is made by turning the slotted screw on the left-hand side of the headlamp rim. Turning this screw clockwise will raise the beam; turning it anticlockwise will lower it.

If it becomes necessary to remove the lamps or replace wiring, the following instructions apply. The headlamp rim and reflector can be removed if the knurled screw is first undone. Removing the three spring clips on the reflector will then enable this component to be parted from the rim and the glass and sealing gasket removed.

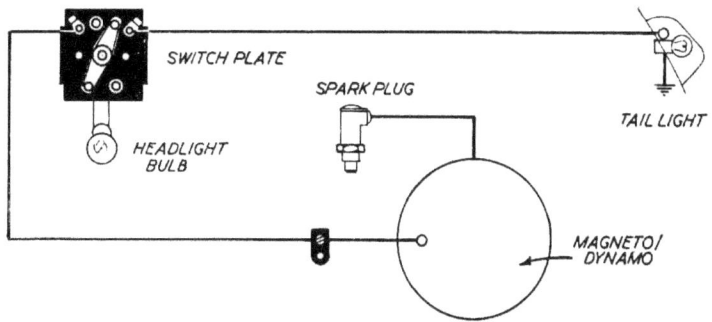

FIG. 55. WIRING DIAGRAM FOR 6-VOLT 3-WATT SYSTEM ON EARLIEST MODELS

To remove the headlamp complete (on Quickly-N and Quickly-S) follow the above by disconnecting both leads. Unscrew the hexagon cap nut on the fork stem and remove the lock washers; then the two hexagon-headed bolts and nuts with their serrated washers between the forks and handlebar bracket so that the complete handlebars can be removed. The lamp can then be taken off.

To remove the headlamp wires only (e.g. to renew the wiring), proceed as in the first paragraph. Disconnect both leads and pull out together with their protective sleeving.

The rear lamp cover is quite simply removed by unscrewing the slotted screw. Disconnecting the lead and unscrewing the nut with lock washer on the mudguard will enable the bulb holder to be removed.

Removal of the rear-light lead is a little more awkward. After disconnecting the lead from the fitting, pull through the mudguard and unclip right back to the frame (bending the clips open to free the lead).

Headlamp and Horn: Quickly F. The headlamp assembly is released by undoing the two slotted screws when the whole assembly can be pulled out forwards. The assembly can then be removed completely, if necessary by disconnecting the cables.

To remove the headlamp mounting shell, remove the headlamp

complete, as above, and unscrew the speedometer drive. The shell can then be removed by undoing the slotted screws.

When reassembling, make sure that the earth cable is held securely by spring pressure behind the adjustment screw. Also if the speedometer drive has been removed, make sure that this repositions correctly.

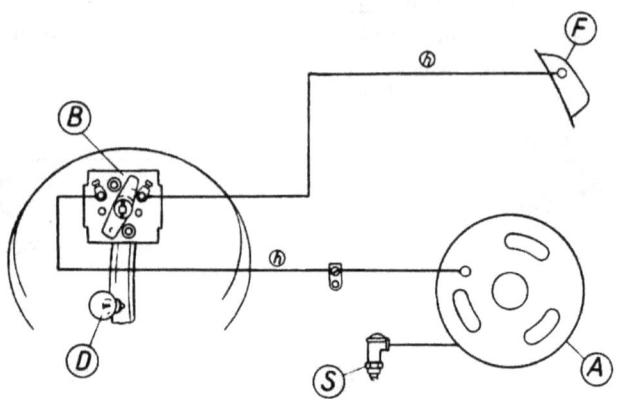

FIG. 56. WIRING DIAGRAM FOR QUICKLY S23, S2 23 AND F
A. Flywheel magneto. B. Light switch. D. Headlamp bulb. F. Tail-light bulb. S. Spark plug.

The horn is removed simply by disconnecting the cables at the horn terminal and unscrewing the nut holding the horn in place. Access to the horn is gained by removing the headlamp and headlamp mounting shell, as described above.

Appendix 1 Specification

Manufacturers. NSU Werke, Aktiengesellschaft, Neckarsulm, Germany.
British and Commonwealth Distributors. NSU (Great Britain) Ltd., 7 Chesterfield Gardens, Curzon Street, London, W.1. (Telephone: GROsvenor 4446-7-8).

Quickly N, S and L Models
  Engine. Two-stroke, light alloy construction with hard-chromed bore.
    Bore, 40 mm (1·575 in.)
    Stroke, 39 mm (1·535 in.)
    Capacity, 49 c.c. (2·99 cu in.)
    Head volume, 10·9 c.c. (0·67 cu in.)
    Compression ratio, 5·5:1
    Maximum B.H.P., 1·4 metric H.P. (1·39 B.H.P. (English))
    Maximum engine speed, 5,500 r.p.m.
    Piston clearance, 0·015 mm–0·025 mm (0·0006–0·001 in.)
    Gudgeon pin diameter, 10 mm–0·05 mm (0·394 in.–0·002 in.)
    Little end diameter, 10 mm $\begin{Bmatrix} + 0.028 \text{ mm} \\ - 0.013 \text{ mm} \end{Bmatrix}$ $\left(0.394 \text{ in.} \begin{Bmatrix} + 0.001 \text{ in.} \\ - 0.005 \text{ in.} \end{Bmatrix} \right)$
    Maximum axial crankshaft play, 0·3 mm (0·012 in.).
  Fuel. Petroil mixture, 1 part SAE 50 oil to 24 parts petrol (equivalent practical mixture ⅓ pint SAE 50 per Imperial gallon of petrol).
  Fuel Tank Capacity
  $\begin{Bmatrix} 3 \cdot 1 \text{ litres } (5\frac{1}{2} \text{ pints}) \text{ or} \\ 4 \cdot 46 \text{ litres } (8 \text{ pints})\text{—new models} \end{Bmatrix}$ which includes 0·4 litres (¾ pint) reserve.
  Overall Dimensions
    Maximum height of machine, 960 mm (37¾ in.)
    Maximum width, 642 mm (25¼ in.)
    Length, 1,895 mm (74½ in.)
    Height of saddle, 780 mm (30¾ in.), adjustable.
  Frame. Pressed-steel beam type, welded assembly.
  Wheels. Rims, 26 × 2 well-base rims.
    Spokes, front wheel, L.H. 263 mm × 2·65 mm diam (10⅜ in. × ¹⁄₁₀ in.)
              R.H. 235 mm × 2·65 mm diam (9¼ in. × ¹⁄₁₀ in.)
         rear wheel, L.H. 235 mm × 3·0 mm diam (9¼ in. × 0·118 in.)
              R.H. 263 mm × 3·0 mm diam (10⅜ in. × 0·118 in.).

Brakes. Internal expanding type, both wheels.
Front brake cable-operated by hand lever.
Back brake (Quickly-N and Quickly-S) rod-operated via back-pedalling.
(Quickly-L) Bowden cable, operated via back-pedalling.

Carburettor. Bing type 1/9/1.
Main jet, No. 56
Needle jet, 2·10
Needle position, 2.

Clutch. Multi-plate type.
Spring pressure, 47·5 kg (105 lb).

Gearbox. Two-speed gearbox built integral with engine unit.
Reduction—engine : gearbox, 5·33:1
gearbox : rear wheels, 3:1
gearbox ratios, 1·88:1
1:1
overall reduction ratios, 30·06:1 (first gear)
15·99:1 (second gear).

Power Transmission. By chain 12·7 × 4·88 mm pitch, 112 links.
Chain sprockets—rear, 36 teeth
front, 12 teeth (a 13-tooth front chain sprocket is also available as a standard alternative).

Axial Play of Gearbox Shafts. 0·2 mm (0·008 in.).

Ignition. Flywheel magneto-generator 6-volt, 17-watt.
Spark timing, 2·1 mm (0·084 in.) or 24 degrees before top-dead-centre
Contact-breaker gap, 0·2–0·3 mm (0·008–012 in.)
Spark plug (standard), Bosch W 240 T 11 or Bosch W 240 P 11S
British equivalents: KLG F75
Champion L–85
Lodge silver electrode model HH 14
Spark plug gap, 0·5 mm (0·020 in.).

Electrical Equipment.
Dipping headlamp
Tail lamp
Horn.

Quickly S/2 Model

Engine. As for other models (*see* above).
Output 1·7 B.H.P. at 5,100 r.p.m.

Fuel Tank. Complete group like Quickly N and S models.

APPENDIX I: SPECIFICATION 99

Fuel Tank Capacity. 1 gallon approx. (reserve approx. ¼ pint).

Overall Dimensions. Similar to other models (*see* above).

Wheels. 25 × 2·25.

Tyre size. 25 × 2·25.

Tyre Pressures. 15–18 lb front, 32 lb rear—solo.
15–18 lb front, 36 lb rear—two up.

Carburettor. Bing 1/12/127.
  Main jet, 66
  Needle jet, 2·12
  Needle position, 2.

Gearing. Engine: gearbox, 5·33 : 1.
  Gearbox: rear wheel, 3·16 : 1
  Gearbox ratios, 2·44 : 1 (1st gear)
              1·563 : 1 (2nd gear)
              1 : 1 (3rd gear).

  Overall ratios, 41·1 : 1 (1st gear)
              26·4 : 1 (2nd gear)
              16·84 : 1 (3rd gear).

Approximate Speed in Gears. 5–15 m.p.h. (1st gear)
              10–25 m.p.h. (2nd gear)
              15–35 m.p.h. (3rd gear).

Speedometer Group (comprising speedometer head, spring, flexible drive, speedometer drive and felt washer) is special to the S/2.

Exhaust System. Complete exhaust system like N and S models.

Electrical System (including headlamp, rear light, and cable harness).
  Complete group like Quickly N and S models, as for other models *see* above.

Special Equipment (available for S/2).
  Leg cowling
  Tyre pump
  Luggage carrier.

Overall Dimensions. Similar to other models (*see* above).

Unladen weight. 110 lb approx.

Permissible load. 480 lb.

Tools. 1 8 × 9 mm spanner.
      1 10 × 11 mm spanner.
      1 screwdriver.
      1 12 × 19 mm spanner.
      1 box spanner.
      1 pin.

Quickly N 23 Model

Specification is basically similar to that of the Quickly N but with improved mudguard design, improved lights, stronger centre stand and the use of 23-in. wheels. It differs in the following essential details from the Quickly S 23.

    (i) The tool-kit cover is released by inserting a small coin in the slotted screw-head on the cover on the front fork cowling and unscrewing a few turns.

    (ii) The pump is fixed on the luggage-carrier stay.

    (iii) The bolt on the rear end of the headlight body serves for adjusting the headlamp beam. Turn this bolt to the left or right until the beam strikes the ground approximately 10 yards ahead of the front wheel.

Engine. Single-cylinder, two-stroke.
    Bore, 40 mm.
    Stroke, 39 mm.
    Capacity, 49 c.c.
    Compression ratio, 5·5:1.

Gear Ratios. 1st gear: 1·88:1.
                 2nd gear: 1:1.

Carburettor. Bing 1/9/22.
          Main jet 56.
          Needle jet 210.
          Needle setting 3.

Dimensions. Height overall $37\frac{1}{2}$ in.
           Length overall $72\frac{1}{2}$ in.
           Width overall $25\frac{1}{4}$ in.

Tyres. 23 × 2·00 in.
    Maximum permissible all-up weight 287 lb.

Quickly S 23, Quickly S/2 23 and Quickly F

Specification for these models is basically similar to that of the Quickly S/2, but with 23-in. wheels, larger streamlined fuel tank with knee grips, streamlined headlamp and speedometer fairing.

Engine. Single-cylinder, two-stroke.
    Bore, 40 mm. diam.

APPENDIX I: SPECIFICATION

Stroke, 39 mm.
Capacity, 49 c,c.
Compression ratio, 6·8:1.
Quickly S, 5·5:1.

Electrical Equipment. Dynamo magneto.
Spark plug, Bosch W 190 M 11 S or a plug with the same qualities.
Headlamp bulb, 17 watts, 6 volts.
Tail-light bulb, 2 watts, 6 volts.

Fuel Unit. Bing starter carburettor, 1/12/117.
Quickly S, 1/9/22.
Carburettor settings:
Main jet, 66.
Quickly S, 54.
Needle jet, 2·1.
Needle setting, 2.
Quickly S, 3.
Amount of fuel in the fuel tank, 1½ gallons.
Fuel reserve, 3½ pints.

Air Filter. In the frame, on the left, above the gearbox.

Chassis. Central pressed frame.
Front, Swinging links on front fork.
Rear, Swinging arm rear suspension.
Gear ratios:
Quickly S.
1st gear, 1·88:1.
2nd gear, 1:1.
Quickly S/2.
1st gear, 2·44:1.
2nd gear, 1·563:1.
3rd gear, 1:1.
Tyres:
Quickly S/2.
Front 23 × 2¼ in.
Rear 23 × 2½ in.,
Quickly S. 23 × 2¼ in.

Braking Area. S 23, 2 × 3·4 sq. in.
S/2 23 and F, 2 × 6·5 sq. in.

General Details. Maximum height overall, 38 in.
Maximum length overall, 7½ in.
Maximum width overall, 25½ in.
Total admissible weight, 485 lb.
Quickly S, 309 lb.

Appendix 2 Design Changes

EACH Quickly machine is designated by two six-figure numbers, separated by an oblique stroke. The first number refers to the frame number and the second to the number of the engine, e.g.

frame number → 482 754/522 989 ← engine number.

In ordering spare parts for any particular machine it is necessary to quote both these numbers and also the model (i.e. Quickly-N, -L or -S).

NSU Spare Parts are coded numerically in four-figure-blocks commencing with 11, 16 or 19, e.g. 16 01 00 034.

Parts made to German DIN standards (the equivalent of our British Standard Specifications, but designated in metric sizes) are designated by their respective DIN numbers and dimensions.

In addition, where parts are plated or otherwise finished, a further code number is added to indicate the type of finish required—

10—chromium plated
31—black
57—dual-tone: jade green pale green
70—dual-tone: light grey, dove grey
73—dual-tone: lido blue, pearl grey
74—dual-tone: virginia brown, sand
75—dual-tone: whale grey, coral red.

A Spare Parts List is essential to find the appropriate part number for any component. All NSU Dealers hold such a list and can therefore identify the required spare or spares. There are, however, a number of detail design changes affecting components and assemblies where parts have been changed (or omitted). These are listed below for general reference together with the model numbers concerned.

Engine Unit

For models prior to serial number 501 834/545 056, a replacement engine will require boring out of the engine mounting holes in the frame and on the carrying handle to take 8·3 mm bolts. Also removal of the threaded projection on the frame. New bolts, lock washers and nuts will be required to remount the engine. Replacement of a crankcase on engines prior to 545 056 will require similar treatment on frames prior to 501 834.

Replacement of the gearbox layshaft on models prior to 82 401/87 963 requires grinding down the shoulder on the gear wheel for first and second gear by 1 mm and replacing with a 1 mm thick washer.

APPENDIX II: DESIGN CHANGES

Crankcase Assembling Parts
Original design used up to model 193 540/208 745.
(Additional spacer and screw included up to model 62 700/66 989 on chain cover side; and up to model 78 000/82 792 on right side.)
Assembly components changed from model 193 541/208 746 onwards.

Cylinder Head
Original pattern on all models up to 482 754/522 989.
Revised pattern on model 482 755/522 990 and subsequently.
These two parts remain interchangeable.

Carburettor
Original pattern used up to model 482 754/522 989.
Revised pattern on model 482 755/522 990 and subsequently. (This affects only the choke cover plate and gasket.)

Magneto-generator
Bosch LMUP 1/115/17 L 2 on models up to 358 398/377 954.
Bosch LM UPA 1/115/17 L la *or* Noris ELZJ 17/4 on model 358 399/377 955 and subsequently.

Brake Lever (Rear Brake)
Original pattern used up to model 482 754/522 989.
Revised pattern on model 482 755/522 990 and subsequently. The brake lever is a different pattern again for L model.

Frame
Original design up to model 482 754/522 989.
Revised on model 482 755/522 990 and subsequently.
Further modified design on L model.

Saddle
Original pattern used up to model 97 844/104 888.
Design changed on model 97 845/104 889 and subsequently.

Luggage Carrier
Original pattern used on models up to 208 884/225 051.
Changed on model 208 885/225 052 and subsequently.

Silencer Assembly
Original pattern used up to model 103 080/109 872 with minor detail differences.
Modified design introduced on model 331 789/349 436 and subsequently.

Front Forks
Original pattern used up to model 109 741/117 525.
Modified pattern introduced on model 109 742/117 526 up to model 482 754/522 989.
Revised design introduced on model 482 755/522 990 and subsequently.

Handlebar Assembly
   Original pattern used up to model 482 754/522 989.
   Revised design introduced on model 482 755/522 990 and subsequently

Speedometer
   Original pattern used up to model 281 717/299 049.
   Revised pattern used on models 281 718/299 050 to 482 754/522 989.
   Revised pattern fitted to model 482 755/522 990 and subsequently.

Engine/Frame Number Series
   Quickly-N from 000 001/000 001.
   Quickly-S from 360 030/380 173.
   Quickly-L from 530 211/576 197.
   Cavallino from 668 411/704 717.
   Quickly-T from 2 900 001/2 900 041.
   Quickly-TT from 3 900 001/3 900 001.
   Quickly 23-N from 1 050 001/16 41717.
   Quickly 23-S from 1 000 001/16 17827.
   Quickly 23-S/2 from 16 20001/39 35 017.
   Quickly 23-F from 1 800 001.

APPENDIX II: DESIGN CHANGES

SUMMARY OF DESIGN CHANGES

Component or Assembly	Up to	Changes (Model Numbers) from
Crankcase		
Bush	164 546/176 279	—
Clevis link	92 805/99 003	--
Assembly parts	193 540/208 745	193 541/208 746
Chain cover spacer	62 700/66 989	eliminated
Right-side cover spacer	78 000/82 792	eliminated
Cylinder Head		
Decompression valve	482 754/522 989	482 755/522 990
Decompression valve assembly	482 754/522 989	482 755/522 990
Carburettor		
Choke cover	482 754/522 989	482 755/522)
Magneto-generator		
Bosch LMUP L2	358 398/377 954	
Bosch LM UPA		358 399/377 955
Gearbox		
Main gear		at 475 572/515 366
Selector pin	92 805/99 003	92 806/99 004
Washers		at 82 400/87 962
		493 384/535 583
Brake lever	482 754/522 989	482 755/522 990
Frame	482 754/522 989	482 755/522 990
Forked pin	360 029/380 172	eliminated
Stem rivet/bolt	360 029/380 172	360 030/380 173
Rubber plug		211 251/226 947
Saddle	97 844/104 888	97 845/104 889
Luggage carrier	208 884/225 051	208 885/225 052
Stand washers	55 200/61 885	55 201/61 836
Mudguard bolts	109 741/117 525	109 742/117 526
Silencer assembly	at 100 081/109 873	
	at 100 500/107 393	
	at 105 060/112 072	
	at 331 789/349 436	
Handlebar assembly		
(N and S models)	482 754/522 989	482 745/522 990
Throttle twistgrip	268 490/286 207	268 491/286 208
	482 754/622 989	482 755/522 990
Gearchange twistgrip	268 490/286 207	268 491/286 208
	482 754/522 989	482 755/522 990
Throttle cable	268 490/286 207	268 491/286 208
	482 754/522 989	482 755/522 990
Gearchange cable	482 754/522 989	482 755/522 990
Decompressor cable	482 754/522 989	482 755/522 990
Front wheel	261 860/279 419	261 861/279 420
	261 860/279 419	261 861/279 420
Hub	482 754/522 989	482 755/522 990
Brake	482 754/522 989	482 755/522 990
Rear wheel	259 464/277 026	259 465/277 027
	482 754/522 989	482 755/522 990
Hub	259 464/277 026	259 465/277 027
Brake	482 754/522 989	482 755/522 027
	482 754/522 989	482 755/522 990
Brake rod assembly	482 754/522 989	482 755/522 990
Headlamp		
N and S models	281 717/209 049	281 718/209 050

Appendix 3 Model Components

SUMMARY OF QUICKLY MODEL COMPONENTS

PART	MODEL							
	N	S	Cavallino	L	S/2	T	TT	F
Engine (with flywheel, generator and carburettor)	✓	✓	✓	✓	✓	✓	✓	✓
Engine group—Crankcase	✓	✓	✓	✓	✓	✓	✓	✓
Cylinder	✓	✓	✓	✓	✓	✓	✓	✓
Cylinder head	✓	✓	✓	✓	✓	✓	✓	✓
Flywheel assembly Crankshaft	✓	✓	✓	✓	✓	✓	✓	✓
Clutch Gearbox	✓	✓	✓	✓	✓	✓	✓	✓
Carburettor	✓	✓	✓	✓	✓	✓	✓	✓
Frame	✓	✓	✓	✓	✓	✓	✓	✓
Wheels	✓	✓	✓	✓	✓	✓	✓	✓

This table details the common and different components applicable throughout the Quickly series.

APPENDIX III: MODEL COMPONENTS

SUMMARY OF QUICKLY-S/2 COMPONENTS

Component	Comments
Engine: Crankshaft	Complete group as Quickly-T
	R.H. cover as Quickly-TT
Cylinder	Complete group as Quickly-TT
Crankshaft	Complete group as Quickly-TT
Gearbox	Complete group as Quickly-T with new pedal cranks
Clutch	Complete group as Quickly-T
Carburettor	As for Quickly-TT
Frame	Specific to S/2
Front mudguard*	As Quickly-L with detail differences
Rear mudguard*	Specific to S/2
Dual seat	Specific to S/2
Centre stand	As Quickly-TT
Spring fork*	Specific to S/2
Handlebar assembly*	Basically as for Quickly-TT
Front wheel	Specific to S/2 (hub as Quickly-T
Rear wheel	Specific to S/2
Foot brake	Basically as Quickly N-S
Chain drive	Specific to S/2
Exhaust system	Complete group as Quickly N-S
Fuel tank	Complete group as Quickly N-S
Electrical system	Complete group as Quickly N-S

* Other parts as for Quickly N and S

SUMMARY OF QUICKLY 23-inch WHEEL MODELS
(Quickly S/2, S 23 and F)

Component	Comments
Engine	Basically same as Quickly S/2
Gearbox (S 23)	Basically same as Quickly-S
(S/2 23 and F)	Basically same as Quickly S/2
Clutch	Five-plate clutch on all late models
Carburettor	As for Quickly S/2 with larger jets and longer intake gasket
Frame (S/2 23 and S 23)	Specific for 23-in. wheel models
(F)	Specific to F with pivoted rear suspension
Mudguards, Front and Rear	Specific to 23-in. wheel models
Centre stand	Strengthened, and specific to new models
Front wheel	23 × $2\frac{1}{4}$ in.
Rear wheel (S 23)	23 × $2\frac{3}{4}$ in.
(S/2 23 and F)	23 × $2\frac{1}{2}$ in.
Footbrake: (S 23)	Basically as Quickly
(S/1 23)	Specific to S/2 23
(F)	Specific to F
Tank	New styling and specific to 23-in. wheel models (except N-23).
Electrical system	Basically as S/2 (modified headlamp group)

Appendix 4 Special Tools

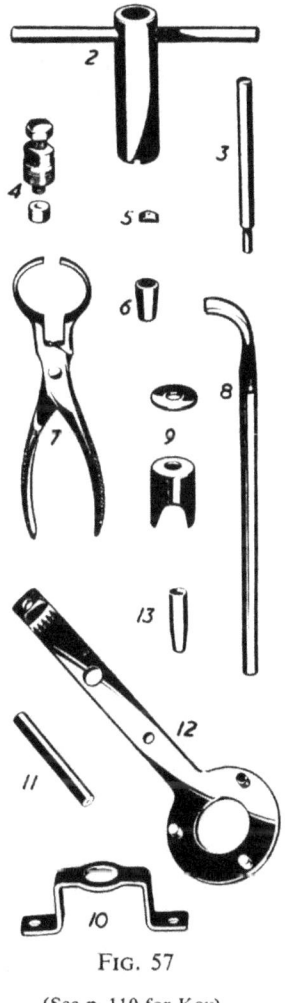

Fig. 57

(See p. 110 for Key)

(FIG. 57)

Fig. Reference	Description	Use	NSU Parts Number
1*	Engine clamping fixture	Bench mounting engine	16 91 00 901
2	Box spanner	Pedal crank spindle nuts	16 91 00 902
3	Punch	Extraction of gudgeon pin	16 91 00 903
4	Extractor	Extraction of flywheel	16 91 00 904
5	Filler piece	,, ,, ,,	16 91 00 905
6	Tapered sleeve	For fitting left-hand end of pedal crank spindle	16 91 00 906
7	Piston-ring pliers	Assembly of piston rings	16 91 00 907
8	Levers (2 reqd.)	For removing clutch cap	16 91 00 908
9	Sleeve	For assembling inner clutch casing	16 91 00 909
10	Bracket	Assembly bracket for clutch spring	16 91 00 910
11	Setting pin	Con rod	16 91 00 911
12	Holder	For holding rotor and intermediate gear	16 91 00 913
13	Tapered sleeve	Assembly of crankcase	01 81 10 282
	Complete set of special tools		16 91 00 914

* Not illustrated.

Index

AIR filter, 66, 70

BACK pedalling, 15
Brake cable, see Cables
Brake specification, 98, 101
Brakes, 47 et seq.
Braking, 26
British agents, 2

CABLES, 42–6, 61, 62
Carburettor, 9, 66 et seq.
  S/2, 68
  23 models, 69
  specification, 98–100
Chain, 15, 31, 32, 64
Chain tension, 32
Changing gear, 13
Choke, 23, 68
Choke cable, see Cables
Clutch, 10, 12, 27, 83, 89
Clutch cable, see Cables
Clutch spring pressure, 98
Components, 106, 107
Condenser, 91–2
Contact breaker, 72–3, 91, 98, 100
Controls, 21, 22
Cooling, 8
Crankcase components, 77
Cylinder head removal, 84, 86

DECARBONIZING, 86–8
Decompressor, 9, 43, 46, 88
Design changes, 102–4
Driving technique, 24–7
Dynamo, see Magneto/generator
Dynamo circuit, 91

ELECTRICAL equipment, 90–5
Engine components, 78
  number series, 104
  specification, 97, 100
  unit, 73–86
Equipment, 16

FAULT finding, 39–41, 89
Flywheel, 71–2

Frame, 1, 8
  numbers, 104
Front brake, 47–51
Front forks, see Spring fork
Front hub, 49–51
Fuel mixture, 18, 19, 97
Fuel tank, 97–8, 101
Fuel tap, 19, 20, 27

GEAR changing, 25, 26
Gearbox, 12, 13, 14
  two-speed, 79
  three-speed, 80
Gearchange cable, 47

HANDLEBARS, 22, 61, 62
Headlamp—
  adjustment, 94–5
  bulb, 93

LIGHTS, 93
Lighting circuits, 94, 95
Lubricating oils, 30
Lubrication, 29 et seq.
Lubrication points, 30
Lubrication table, 37–8

MAGNETO circuit, 91
Magneto/generator, 71–3
Maintenance—
  weekly, 32
  monthly, 33
  three-monthly, 34
  six-monthly, 35
Mixture setting, 66–7
Moped production, v, 1

NSU—
  agents (G.B.), 2
  factory, 1, 2
  models,
    Cavallino, 4, 6
    F, 7
    L, 4, 5, 6
    N, 4

NSU—
  models (*contd.*)—
    N/23, 7, 8
    S, 4, 5
    S/2, 6, 7
    S/2 23, 6, 8
    T, TT, 4, 6, 7

PEDAL drive, 14, 15
Petrol mixture, 18, 19, 97
Petrol tank, 19, 97, 98, 101
Petrol tap, 19, 20, 27

REAR brake, 47, 52–4, 56
Reassembling engine, 81–4
Regrinding valve, 88
Replacement engine parts, 84
Replacing bulbs, 95
Running in, 29, 31

SADDLE adjustment, 17, 18
Silencer, 87
Spark plug, 92, 98, 100
Spark plug gap, 98, 100
Spark timing, *see* Timing
Special tools, 109–10
Specifications, 97–101

Speedometer, 55, 99
Speedometer drive, 56
Spring fork, 58–60
Starting, 23 *et seq.*
Stator, 72, 90
Steering head, 58–9, 60, 63
Stripping engine, 75 *et seq.*

TAIL lamp bulb, 93
Throttle cable, *see* Cables
Throttle control, late models, 46
Tickler, 21, 23
Timing, 72, 98, 100
Tools, S/2, 100
Trouble shooting, 39–41
Twistgrips, 44–5
Two-stroke principles, 8
Tyre pressures—
  S/2, 99

VIBRATION, 89

WHEEL stand, 75
Wheels, 48, 56, 97, 99
Wiring diagram (early model), 95
Wiring diagrams (L, N *and* S), 94

AUTOBOOKS WORKSHOP MANUALS

ALFA ROMEO GIULIA 1300, 1600, 1750, 2000 1962-1978 WSM
BMW 1600 1966-1973 WSM
BMW 2000 & 2002 1966-1976 WSM
BMW 2500, 2800, 3.0 & 3.3 1968-1977 WSM
BMW 316, 320, 320i 1975-1977 WSM
BMW 518, 520, 520i 1973-1981 WSM
FIAT 1100, 1100D, 1100R & 1200 1957-1969 WSM
FIAT 124 1966-1974 WSM
FIAT 124 SPORT 1966-1975 WSM
FIAT 125 & 125 SPECIAL 1967-1973 WSM
FIAT 126, 126L, 126 DV, 126/650 & 126/650 DV 1972-1982 WSM
FIAT 127 SALOON, SPECIAL & SPORT, 900, 1050 1971-1981 WSM
FIAT 128 1969-1982 WSM
FIAT 1300, 1500 1961-1967 WSM
FIAT 131 MIRAFIORI 1975-1982 WSM
FIAT 132 1972-1982 WSM
FIAT 500 1957-1973 WSM
FIAT 600, 600D & MULTIPLA 1955-1969 WSM
FIAT 850 1964-1972 WSM
JAGUAR E-TYPE 1961-1972 WSM
JAGUAR MK 1, 2 1955-1969 WSM
JAGUAR S TYPE, 420 1963-1968 WSM
JAGUAR XK 120, 140, 150 MK 7, 8, 9 1948-1961 WSM
LAND ROVER 1, 2 1948-1961 WSM
MERCEDES-BENZ 190 1959-1968 WSM
MERCEDES-BENZ 220/8 1968-1972 WSM
MERCEDES-BENZ 220B 1959-1965 WSM
MERCEDES-BENZ 230 1963-1968 WSM
MERCEDES-BENZ 250 1968-1972 WSM
MERCEDES-BENZ 280 1968-1972 WSM
MG MIDGET TA-TF 1936-1955 WSM
MINI 1959-1980 WSM
MORRIS MINOR 1952-1971 WSM
PEUGEOT 404 1960-1975 WSM
PORSCHE 911 1964-1973 WSM
PORSCHE 911 1970-1977 WSM
RENAULT 16 1965-1979 WSM
RENAULT 8, 10, 1100 1962-1971 WSM
ROVER 3500, 3500S 1968-1976 WSM
SUNBEAM RAPIER, ALPINE 1955-1965 WSM
TRIUMPH SPITFIRE, GT6, VITESSE 1962-1968 WSM
TRIUMPH TR2, TR3, TR3A 1952-1962 WSM
TRIUMPH TR4, TR4A 1961-1967 WSM
VOLKSWAGEN BEETLE 1968-1977 WSM

VELOCEPRESS AUTOMOBILE BOOKS & MANUALS

ABARTH BUYERS GUIDE
AUSTIN-HEALEY 6-CYLINDER WSM
AUSTIN-HEALEY SPRITE & MG MIDGET 1958-1971 WSM
BMW 600 LIMOUSINE FACTORY WSM
BMW 600 LIMOUSINE OWNERS HAND BOOK & SERVICE MANUAL
BMW ISETTA FACTORY WSM
BOOK OF THE CARRERA PANAMERICANA - MEXICAN ROAD RACE
COMPLETE CATALOG OF JAPANESE MOTOR VEHICLES
DIALED IN - THE JAN OPPERMAN STORY
FERRARI 250/GT SERVICE AND MAINTENANCE
FERRARI 308 SERIES BUYER'S AND OWNER'S GUIDE
FERRARI BERLINETTA LUSSO
FERRARI BROCHURES AND SALES LITERATURE 1946-1967
FERRARI BROCHURES AND SALES LITERATURE 1968-1989
FERRARI GUIDE TO PERFORMANCE
FERRARI OPP, MAINTENANCE & SERVICE H/BOOKS 1948-1963
FERRARI OWNER'S HANDBOOK
FERRARI SERIAL NUMBERS PART I - ODD NUMBERS TO 21399
FERRARI SERIAL NUMBERS PART II - EVEN NUMBERS TO 1050
FERRARI SPYDER CALIFORNIA
FERRARI TUNING TIPS & MAINTENANCE TECHNIQUES
HENRY'S FABULOUS MODEL "A" FORD
HOW TO BUILD A FIBERGLASS CAR
HOW TO BUILD A RACING CAR
HOW TO RESTORE THE MODEL 'A' FORD
IF HEMINGWAY HAD WRITTEN A RACING NOVEL
JAGUAR E-TYPE 3.8 & 4.2 WSM
LE MANS 24 (THE BOOK THAT THE FILM WAS BASED ON)
MASERATI BROCHURES AND SALES LITERATURE
MASERATI OWNER'S HANDBOOK
METROPOLITAN FACTORY WSM
MGA & MGB OWNERS HANDBOOK & WSM
OBERT'S FIAT GUIDE
PERFORMANCE TUNING THE SUNBEAM TIGER
PORSCHE 356 1948-1965 WSM
PORSCHE 912 WSM
SOUPING THE VOLKSWAGEN
TRIUMPH TR2, TR3, TR4 1953-1965 WSM
VEDA ORR'S NEW REVISED HOT ROD PICTORIAL
VOLKSWAGEN TRANSPORTER, TRUCKS, STATION WAGONS WSM
VOLVO 1944-1968 ALL MODELS WSM

BROOKLANDS BOOKS & ROAD TEST PORTFOLIOS (RTP)

AC CARS 1904-2009
ALFA ROMEO 1920-1933 ROAD TEST PORTFOLIO
ALFA ROMEO 1934-1940 ROAD TEST PORTFOLIO
BRABHAM RALT HONDA THE RON TAURANAC STORY
BUGATTI TYPE 10 TO TYPE 40 ROAD TEST PORTFOLIO
BUGATTI TYPE 10 TO TYPE 251 ROAD TEST PORTFOLIO
BUGATTI TYPE 41 TO TYPE 55 ROAD TEST PORTFOLIO
BUGATTI TYPE 57 TO TYPE 251 ROAD TEST PORTFOLIO
DELAHAYE ROAD TEST PORTFOLIO
FERRARI ROAD CARS 1946-1956 ROAD TEST PORTFOLIO
FIAT 500 1936-1972 ROAD TEST PORTFOLIO
FIAT DINO ROAD TEST PORTFOLIO
HISPANO SUIZA ROAD TEST PORTFOLIO
HONDA ST1100/ST1300 PAN EUROPEAN 1990-2002 RTP
JAGUAR MK1 & MK2 ROAD TEST PORTFOLIO
LOTUS CORTINA ROAD TEST PORTFOLIO
MV AGUSTA F4 750 & 1000 1997-2007 ROAD TEST PORTFOLIO
TATRA CARS ROAD TEST PORTFOLIO

VELOCEPRESS MOTORCYCLE BOOKS & MANUALS

AJS SINGLES & TWINS 250cc THRU 1000cc 1932-1948 (BOOK OF)
AJS SINGLES 1955-65 350cc & 500cc (BOOK OF)
AJS SINGLES 1945-60 350cc & 500cc MODELS 16 & 18 (BOOK OF)
ARIEL 1939-1960 4 STROKE SINGLES (BOOK OF)
ARIEL LEADER & ARROW 1958-1964 (BOOK OF)
ARIEL MOTORCYCLES 1933-1951 WSM
ARIEL PREWAR MODELS 1932-1939 (BOOK OF)
BMW M/CYCLES R26 R27 (1956-1967) FACTORY WSM
BMW M/CYCLES R50 R50S R60 R69S (1955-1969) FACTORY WSM
BSA BANTAM (BOOK OF)
BSA ALL FOUR-STROKE SINGLES & V-TWINS 1936-1952 (BOOK OF)
BSA OHV & SV SINGLES - 250cc 1954-1970 (BOOK OF)
BSA OHV & SV SINGLES 1945-54 250-600cc (BOOK OF)
BSA OHV SINGLES 350 & 500cc 1955-1967 (BOOK OF)
BSA PRE-WAR MODELS TO 1939 (BOOK OF)
BSA TWINS 1948-1962 (BOOK OF)
BSA TWINS 1962-1969 (SECOND BOOK OF)
CATALOG OF BRITISH MOTORCYCLES (1951 MODELS)
DOUGLAS PRE-WAR ALL MODELS 1929-1939 (BOOK OF)
DOUGLAS POST-WAR ALL MODELS 1948-1957 FACTORY WSM
DUCATI 160cc, 250cc & 350cc OHC MODELS FACTORY WSM
HONDA 50 ALL MODELS UP TO 1970 INC MONKEY & TRAIL (BOOK OF)
HONDA 90 ALL MODELS UP TO 1966 (BOOK OF)
HONDA MOTORCYCLES 125-150 TWINS C/CS/CB/CA WSM
HONDA MOTORCYCLES 250-305 TWINS C/CS/CB WSM
HONDA MOTORCYCLES C100 SUPER CUB WSM
HONDA MOTORCYCLES C110 SPORT CUB 1962-1969 WSM
HONDA TWINS & SINGLES 50cc THRU 305cc 1960-1966 (BOOK OF)
HONDA TWINS ALL MODELS 125cc THRU 450cc UP TO 1968 (BOOK OF)
INDIAN PONYBIKE, BOY RACER & PAPOOSE ILL PARTS LIST & SALES LIT
LAMBRETTA ALL 125 & 150cc MODELS 1947-1957 (BOOK OF)
LAMBRETTA LI & TV MODELS 1957-1970 (SECOND BOOK OF)
MATCHLESS 350 & 500cc SINGLES 1945-1956 (BOOK OF)
MATCHLESS 350 & 500cc SINGLES 1955-1966 (BOOK OF)
NORTON 1938-1956 (BOOK OF)
NORTON DOMINATOR TWINS 1955-1965 (BOOK OF)
NORTON MODELS 19, 50 & ES2 1955-1963 (BOOK OF)
NORTON MOTORCYCLES 1957-1970 FACTORY WSM
NORTON PREWAR MODELS 1932-1939 (BOOK OF)
NSU QUICKLY ALL MODELS 1953-1963 (BOOK OF)
ROYAL ENFIELD SINGLES & V TWINS 1937-1953 (BOOK OF)
ROYAL ENFIELD 736cc INTERCEPTOR FACTORY WSM
ROYAL ENFIELD 250cc & 350cc SINGLES 1958-1966 (SECOND BOOK OF)
SUZUKI 50cc & 80cc UP TO 1966 (BOOK OF)
SUZUKI T10 1963-1967 FACTORY WSM
SUZUKI T20 & T200 1965-1969 FACTORY WSM
TRIUMPH PRE-WAR MOTORCYCLE 1935-1939 (BOOK OF)
TRIUMPH MOTORCYCLES 1937-1951 WSM
TRIUMPH MOTORCYCLES 1945-1955 FACTORY WSM
TRIUMPH TWINS 1956-1969 (BOOK OF)
VELOCETTE ALL SINGLES & TWINS 1925-1970 (BOOK OF)
VESPA 1951-1961 (BOOK OF)
VESPA 125 & 150cc & GS MODELS 1955-1963 (SECOND BOOK OF)
VESPA 90, 125 & 150cc 1963-1972 (THIRD BOOK OF)
VESPA GS & SS 1955-1968 (BOOK OF)
VINCENT MOTORCYCLES 1935-1955 WSM

**PLEASE VISIT OUR WEBSITE
www.VelocePress.com
FOR A DETAILED DESCRIPTION
OF ANY OF THESE TITLES**

Please check our website:

www.VelocePress.com

for a complete
up-to-date list of
available titles

www.ingramcontent.com/pod-product-compliance
Lightning Source LLC
Chambersburg PA
CBHW060349190426
43201CB00043B/1868